CHASING THE SUN

CHASING THE SUN

Rethinking
East Asian Policy

MORTON ABRAMOWITZ AND STEPHEN BOSWORTH

A CENTURY FOUNDATION BOOK

The Century Foundation Press   •   New York

The Century Foundation sponsors and supervises timely analyses of economic policy, foreign affairs, and domestic political issues. Not-for-profit and nonpartisan, it was founded in 1919 and endowed by Edward A. Filene.

LIBRARY OF CONGRESS CATALOGING-IN-PUBLICATION DATA

Abramowitz, Morton, 1933–
  Chasing the sun : rethinking East Asian policy / Morton Abramowitz and Stephen Bosworth.
    p. cm.
  Includes index.
  ISBN-13: 978-0-87078-500-9 (pbk. : alk. paper)
  ISBN-10: 0-87078-500-1 (pbk. : alk. paper)
  ISBN-13: 978-0-87078-504-7 (cloth : alk. paper)
  ISBN-10: 0-87078-504-4 (cloth : alk. paper)
  1. East Asia—Foreign relations—United States. 2. United States—Foreign relations—East Asia. 3. East Asia—Politics and government—20th century. 4. East Asia—Politics and government—21st century. 5. Regionalism—East Asia. 6. United States—Foreign relations—1989– I. Bosworth, Stephen W. II. Title.
  DS518.8.A69 2006
  327.7305—dc22

                                                         2006009166

Cover design and illustration by Claude Goodwin.
Manufactured in the United States of America.
East Asia map, page x, © 2006 Current History, Inc.

FOREWORD

The long day wanes for American preeminence in East Asia. The growing ability of Asians to shape their own future is occurring not primarily as a result of a weakening of the United States. America, in fact, remains uniquely powerful. But it is not omnipotent, and probably not even as strong, relatively, as it was just a decade or two ago. The accumulation of national debt owed abroad—particularly to East Asia—and the sharply unfavorable balance of payments, for example, could have negative consequences for the American economy. America's enormous military strength is currently stretched thin, with major forces pinned down by vexing commitments in the Middle East and Afghanistan. American political will and priorities, too, have altered, toward an obvious preoccupation with new threats and areas of tension.

The changes pale, however, relative to the effects of rapid and sweeping developments in East Asia. The region's economic transformation and political evolution in recent decades are changing the U.S.–East Asia relationship in fundamental ways, and indeed will have global implications for generations to come. Extrapolation is always perilous as a method of predicting the future, but the trends in Asia, particularly when you add India into the equation, suggest that the geopolitical map of the world is being reshaped. We may well be living through the early years of what will come to be known as the Asian Century.

American leaders, of course, are aware of these important shifts in economic and political power, even though they are often preoccupied with more pressing and troubling matters. In fact, before September 11, the Bush administration considered tough responses to the rise of China to be among the greatest policy priorities. Today, however, the basic fact of American foreign policy is that heightened concerns about terrorism and relations with the Muslim world have taken precedence over just about any other matters of state. This work is a reminder that, however great the threat of terrorism, there are forces under way in Asia that the United States cannot afford to ignore.

With more than half the world's population—four times that of the United States, Western Europe, and Japan combined—the developing countries of East and South Asia may well come to dominate the world economy. China, for example, which in 1960 experienced the most catastrophic famine the world has ever seen, forty years later was growing faster economically than any country ever has before. Today, East Asia (excluding Japan) produces about 6 percent of world GDP, while the United States alone produces 28 percent. But Chinese production is doubling roughly every seven years. Projecting current trends, within three to four decades, China is likely to pass the United States as the biggest economy in the world.

The other substantial countries of the East are not yet giant economies, but there is no reason to think they will not attain that status in the years ahead. The world will be quite different if the time comes when Indonesia, Vietnam, Pakistan, Bangladesh, Thailand, the Philippines—each one of which is more populous than France, Britain, or Italy—realize their full economic potential. Indeed, the economic potential of Asia is so great and growth is so rapid that the United States must come to terms with an almost inevitable shift in the global balance of power.

Dynamic economic growth in East Asia is raising hundreds of millions of people out of dire poverty, but it is also creating profound inequalities. In China, for example, this means sharp differences between city and countryside, between coastal China and the deep interior, and between a new entrepreneurial class and workers. Everywhere these changes involve new strains on social cohesion. Everywhere, as well, old political certainties are giving way to new realities of power in the twenty-first century.

In the region, Asians are adjusting to change: business sees nothing but opportunity; policymakers adapt to the strategic consequences of the rise of new powers. Meanwhile, Washington seems to be somewhat behind the curve, with its focus largely on traditional security concerns—nuclear weapons in North Korea and Islamists in Indonesia.

How the United States responds to the new East Asia will be crucial. Do we embrace the rules and institutions of the international community—the United Nations, the World Trade Organization, and international human rights law—to prod China and Asia's other rising powers to do the same? Do we confront potential challengers aggressively, before they gain in strength in an effort to lock in the preeminence the United States has enjoyed since 1945?

Given the importance of this topic, The Century Foundation, which has a long history of investigating developments in the region, including Gunnar Myrdal's landmark 1968 study, *Asian Drama*, has once again begun exploring the difficult issues posed by East Asia. In the past few years, we supported Patrick Tyler's *A Great Wall*, which took a look at U.S.-China relations; Selig Harrison's *Korean Endgame*; and the forthcoming examination of Japan by Kenneth Pyle. In the course of these studies, what became clear was that understanding the relationships between the nations of East Asia and the impact of the changes in the region on U.S. policy was critical, and so we were delighted when our senior fellow Morton Abramowitz and Stephen Bosworth, dean of the Fletcher School at Tufts University, offered to explore this central topic in American foreign policy.

As former ambassadors and State Department officials, the authors fully understand the historical context of American power in Asia since World War II. As scholars, researchers, and interviewers, they have remained active in studying the area, devoting time and considerable attention to exploring the sea changes that have taken place in recent years. This report reflects on the uncertain current situation in contrast to what, in retrospect, was probably the heyday of U.S. power in East Asia—a period when the outsized influence and mission of the United States in Asia was taken for granted. America still looms large in Pacific matters, but as they make clear, it will never have the same level of dominance in the region.

In *Chasing the Sun*, Abramowitz and Bosworth have succeeded in producing a book that combines rich detail about the changes in all of East Asia with practical political observations about U.S. policy toward the region. While the analysis is sophisticated and nuanced, the authors have produced something quite different from the usual academic study. This volume is best read as a guide to policymakers and those who would understand the implications for U.S. policy of the rise of these Asian nations. In some areas, notably North Korea, the authors offer explicit and thoughtful new policy proposals. In others, they provide the raw material needed to rethink past policies in light of new realities. Their discussion of China is particularly broad and integrated.

One of the reasons Abramowitz and Bosworth were so successful as diplomats is that they not only effectively represented U.S. interests abroad, they also developed a deep understanding of the areas in which they served. This work continues that record of insight and knowledge. They urge that Asian dynamism be matched by dynamism in American foreign policy, breaking free of old habits and ideologies to deal with the region as it is and is becoming. Reality has a way of catching up with old notions and present myths. The real question, then, is not whether policy will change—it must—but whether the wisdom found in these pages will inform those changes.

On behalf of the Trustees of The Century Foundation, I thank Ambassadors Abramowitz and Bosworth for this timely and wise volume on American foreign policy.

RICHARD C. LEONE, *President*
The Century Foundation
March 2006

CONTENTS

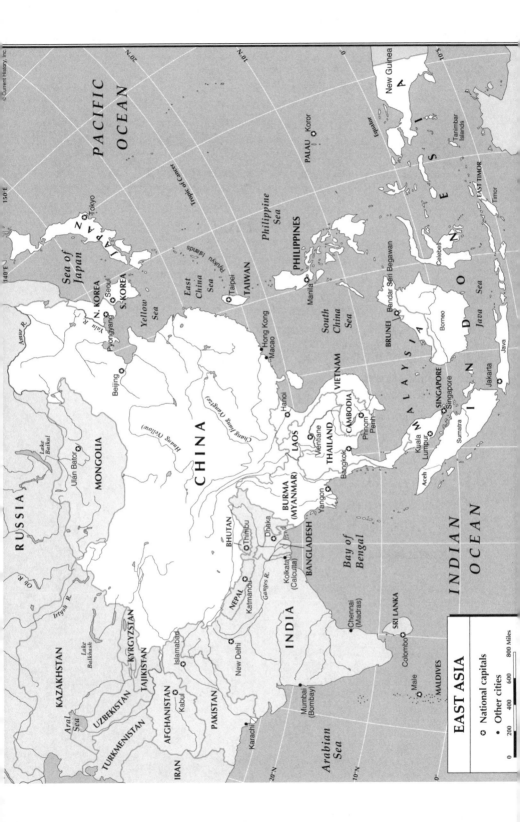

INTRODUCTION

The authors of this book grew up in a half century that had a simple lodestar for American policy in East Asia: prevent the domination of the region by any power other than ourselves.

This dictum turned out to be an effective, if costly, organizing concept for American policy during the cold war. Many U.S. officials still believe in it today; some in the Pentagon argue, for example, that we cannot allow China to begin to challenge our military supremacy in the region. China is considered tolerable as long as it remains a middling military power, cooperates on eliminating North Korea's nuclear threat and rooting out terrorism, unveils its military secrets, avoids trying unilaterally to change the status quo in the Taiwan Strait, and does not challenge the United States in determining the rules of the international road. And if China should stumble a little, that would be okay too.

A cold war framework for American policy, no matter how appealing, however, does not quite work in today's world. Although cold war remnants like North Korea and Taiwan call us back to the twentieth century and American military power in East Asia remains very important, a globalizing world economy, a massively economically and politically transformed—and still changing—East Asia, as well as our own deepening trade and financial interdependence with the region beckon us forward in the twenty-first century. Indeed, many East Asian leaders, while wary of China, fear an American effort to "contain" China that will put them in the middle between a rising regional power and the global superpower. That strategy, they

1

believe, will create dangerous tensions or worse and threaten their golden goose—China's economic engine, which is powering the dramatic advance of the entire region.

In starting this book, we felt reasonably secure that as long-time "Asian hands" we knew something about the region, American interests there, and the policy considerations involved. Both of us have spent much time in East Asia: we each lived there for extended periods and made innumerable trips to the area. During our years in the State Department, we each played parts in some memorable and often dramatic episodes in America's involvement in East Asia: the successful effort to preserve our force structure and bases in the region after the Vietnam War, President Carter's ill-timed and eventually abandoned effort to remove American ground forces from South Korea, the Cambodian war and the flood of refugees from Indochina, the dramatic fall of Philippines President Ferdinand Marcos, the Asian financial crisis of the late nineties, and the emergence of the "Sunshine Policy" of South Korean President Kim Dae Jung. Some of these events have faded in American memories. But memories tend to linger longer in Asia, particularly the unpleasant ones. For example, some well-placed Thais will never understand America's failure to come to their rescue in the 1997 financial crisis.

During the half century of the cold war, the United States was the central player in East Asia. These were heady times for senior American officials working there; not infrequently, American ambassadors were treated as virtual viceroys. Some embraced that role enthusiastically. A few still aspire to it. Despite incessant rhetoric from President Nixon and other senior officials about the awful consequences of American failure in Vietnam, the United States continued to dominate the area even after we abandoned, with little apparent remorse, our Vietnamese, Cambodian, and Lao friends and allies. Among the ironies of that painful engagement is that today Vietnam is closer to the United States than to China, its former ally in war and ideology.

But the era of absolute American preeminence in East Asia is over. The United States remains important, indeed very important, but as one senior Thai official told one of us—somewhat unnecessarily—"Hey, things have changed. We don't have you pro-consuls around anymore. You don't run things here now." Indeed, things have changed beyond our wildest expectations when we were young foreign service officers. Much of that change is positive, and America contributed to it. It is difficult, however, for Americans to get their minds around the magnitude of the change. It continues to surprise both of us and made us rethink some long-held notions about American policies in the area.

In light of East Asia's growing power and influence, the United States needs to consider anew how to help keep the peace and retain influence commensurate with its interests in the region. In our political world, true reassessment is rare, easier to call for than to do. While the landscape is different, much remains that is familiar. The United States cannot avoid its past associations, but it also cannot be bound by outdated pieties. As we manage the legacies of the past, like a still-dangerous North Korea, we also have to understand and deal effectively with the new forces that move events in East Asia, from deepening economic integration to the advance of democracy. The United States faces fundamental questions, most notably, how to sort out its dealings with a dynamic China, something it may not be able to do given the strongly divided views in this country. Sino-American relations obviously require the utmost tending, and the United States has to try to avoid conducting them in the usual piecemeal fashion, despite the vast expansion of our relations with China.

East Asian policy, of course, never stands alone. It is part of a larger global effort. America's efforts in East Asia compete for resources and high-level attention and sometimes conflict with policy on other issues and regions. Since the end of the cold war, all administrations have struggled, unsuccessfully, to find a compelling replacement for the strategy of containment. September 11 produced such a new American strategy, one that shifted our attention and resources to counterterrorism and to the Middle East and diminished emphasis on other regions and on our alliances and international institutions. This shift also has heavily affected our presence and policies in East Asia: the United States moved sizeable military forces out of East Asia, kicked the North Korean nuclear weapons problem down the road, rekindled an interest in Southeast Asia because of the threat from Islamic extremists, and pulled back from a competitive antagonism toward Beijing. Not an inconsequential impact.

Similarly, as a consequence at least in part of our troubled occupation of Iraq, the promotion of democracy has become the central pillar of American foreign policy, certainly rhetorically. So far, however, little seems to have changed in American efforts to promote democracy in East Asia. Giving credibility to this new policy in East Asia will be at least as difficult as in most other regions, particularly where China is concerned. It is easier to beat up on Burma.

Trying to address in a slim volume East Asia's new and old realities, its future direction, and America's policy approach to the region has had its exhilarating moments. It also has tested our imagination and may have exceeded our intellects and certainly the limits of our eloquence. We debated whether so much ground could be usefully covered in a short book. We focused on what we felt were the big issues. That meant we simply dropped some important considerations. For example, we examine the changing political economy of East Asia but provide relatively little discussion of the basic economic issues that receive enormous attention in public policy and business circles. Nor do we discuss important secondary actors such as Australia, Russia, and India, whose influence in Southeast Asia is growing, or delve into issues like public health and energy. We tried to avoid—not always successfully—getting distracted by the flow of day-to-day events.

We concluded that the best approach to getting a decent fix on the present and future problems facing the United States in East Asia was to talk to people in the region—business executives, politicians, officials, academics, and journalists. We spent many weeks in East Asia and talked to hundreds of people. We sought to get our respondents to talk about the trends and issues that preoccupied them and us. We encouraged them to speculate and roam widely in discussing their countries, their concerns, their futures, and what the United States should be doing. Some issues came up everywhere, like the impact of China and East Asia's growing economic integration. We also checked in with lots of knowledgeable Americans and spent much time reading contemporary materials.

From these discussions and our own numerous exchanges, we selected some of the predominant themes in our dealings with East Asia and the issues that should concern Americans—and their policymakers. We turned all this into seven broad essays—long lectures if you will. We start with a brief review of the changing East Asian scene and American policies there, go through the principal issues in greater detail, and end with our thoughts on the policies the United States should pursue in the region.

We came away from our new immersion in East Asia uncertain about the wisdom of some current U.S. policies but on the whole a bit surprised by our optimism. We believe that the potential crises of the Taiwan Strait and North Korea can at least continue to be managed, that nationalism is not predestined to get out of hand, and that China, more likely than not, will continue to concentrate on giving its people a better life. We also find reason for some confidence that China will remain reasonably stable, continue fitfully to become more open, and for the most part eschew the temptation to involve itself unhelpfully in the domestic affairs of its neighbors. Japan's recovered economic vitality may help it become a much more effective diplomatic player in the region. Finally, the outlook for efforts to build something called an East Asian Community is murky indeed, but the economic and political integration of the area continues to gain ground. That is a matter of importance to the United States that gets little attention in U.S. policy circles.

Of course, none of these outcomes are certain or guaranteed; nor are our judgments put forth without some reservations. Some might say our views of the future are unrealistic or even naïve. We would agree that they are unlikely to come to pass without effective policies on the part of the United States.

A new sun has risen in East Asia, and it can make the West uncomfortably warm. American policy in East Asia must be grounded in the region's new realities. The United States cannot allow itself to be mesmerized by military considerations or seduced by excessive geopolitical rhetoric.

March 2006

1

THE NEW EAST ASIA AND AMERICAN INVOLVEMENT

*T*he concept of East Asia—formerly the Far East—as a region began as mostly a Western geographical expression. This area, encompassing the countries from Japan and China through Southeast Asia to Burma, became embedded in the organizational thinking of Western foreign ministries, including the State Department, but East Asia was never a very coherent geographical entity. (Interestingly, the same area was defined before World War II as Japan's Greater East Asia Co-Prosperity Sphere.) To the extent that East Asian countries and peoples had common characteristics, they were mostly the legacy of China's cultural influence and Western imperialism.

Today, however, the expression "East Asia" is a term increasingly discussed in the region and has taken on more concrete significance because of the region's rapidly increasing economic integration and growing self-consciousness. This geographical focus is still, of course, somewhat artificial in today's world: India, outside of East Asia's geographical footprint, is likely to play a much bigger role in the region; Australia and New Zealand are eager to join the East Asian club; Japan and increasingly China are not just East Asian players but world players. Indeed, one of the difficulties East Asian countries have only begun to discuss in their movement toward a more cohesive regional community is whether to include countries outside their current usage of the term East Asia.

Table 1.1. East Asia's Share of World Economy (percent)

	1970	1980	1990	2000	2004
East Asia's Share of World GDP[a]	11.94	14.30	19.49	23.42	20.07
Breakdown of East Asia's Share					
China share	26.51	12.03	8.39	14.62	20.10
Japan share	59.21	67.94	71.91	64.19	56.35
Rest of East Asia	14.29	20.03	19.70	21.19	23.55
East Asia's Share of World Exports[b]	10.93	14.48	21.13	26.32	26.37
Breakdown of East Asia's Share					
China share	7.05	6.64	8.83	14.85	24.86
Japan share	59.04	47.86	40.88	28.56	23.70
Rest of East Asia	33.91	45.50	50.29	56.59	51.44
East Asia's Share of World Imports	11.56	14.78	19.09	22.78	23.29
Breakdown of East Asia's Share					
China share	6.46	6.89	8.15	15.04	25.83
Japan share	53.49	48.84	35.98	25.35	20.94
Rest of East Asia	40.05	44.27	55.87	59.61	53.23
East Asia's Share of World Foreign Direct Investment Inflows (FDI)[c]	5.45	6.83	11.27	10.54	21.25
Breakdown of East Asia's Share					
China share	—	1.51	14.89	27.67	44.02
Japan share	12.85	7.39	7.48	5.66	5.67
Rest of East Asia	87.15	91.10	77.63	66.67	50.30

East Asia is now an international economic power. (See Table 1.1.) Its companies are serious, often dominant, players in virtually every industry. East Asian brands are now global brands. Commodity markets are shaking from the repercussions of East Asia's growth and its escalating demand for energy, steel, aluminum, lumber, and countless other resources. The world's nonagricultural labor force has virtually doubled in only a decade or two as East Asian workers have entered the global economy. East Asia's share of global GDP has risen sharply from nearly 12 percent in 1970 to some 20 percent in 2004. Its share of global exports has grown even more rapidly, from 12 percent in 1975 to 25 percent in 2003. Finally—some would say alarmingly—East Asian central banks now hold some $2 trillion in American assets. Who would have predicted, even ten years ago, that East Asia would become the largest foreign creditor of the United States?

TABLE 1.1. (CONTINUED)

	1970	1980	1990	2000	2004
EAST ASIA'S SHARE OF INTERNATIONAL RESERVES (MINUS GOLD)[d]	—	—	30.62	51.68	63.34
BREAKDOWN OF EAST ASIA'S SHARE					
China share	—	4.77	10.59	16.48	27.25
Japan share	51.97	46.20	28.10	34.77	36.98
Rest of East Asia	48.03	49.03	61.31	48.78	35.77

Note: East Asia is defined as ASEAN Plus Three, Hong Kong, and Taiwan. All amounts calculated in current U.S. dollars.

[a] GDP data unavailable for Brunei, Burma, Cambodia (1980), Laos (1970, 1980), and Vietnam (1970, 1980).

[b] Export and import data unavailable for Brunei, Cambodia (1980, 1990), and Vietnam (1970, 1980, 1990).

[c] FDI data unavailable for Cambodia (1970, 1980), China (1970), and Laos (1970, 1980).

[d] International reserve data unavailable for Brunei, Cambodia (1970, 1980, 1990), China (1970), Hong Kong (1970, 1980), Laos (1970, 1980), and Vietnam (1970, 1980, 1990).

Source: GDP and international reserve calculations based on data from World Bank, *World Bank Development Indicators, 2005*. Trade calculations based on data from International Monetary Fund, *International Financial Statistics, 2005*. FDI calculations based on data from UNCTAD, *Foreign Direct Investment On-line*, available online at http://www.unctad.org. Data for Taiwan from *Statistical Yearbook for the Republic of China 2004*, available online at http://eng.stat.gov.tw.

These massive changes have taken place over only half a century, a remarkably brief period. The ghosts of Western imperialism may linger here and there, but for the most part they have faded away. (The ghosts of Japanese imperialism, on the other hand, are still all too present and haunt Tokyo's relations with its neighbors, especially China and the two Koreas.) Progress, of course, has been uneven. A few economies still lag badly; some governments are unstable; two are very unedifying; and in many countries, including China, a big chunk of the population remains desperately poor. But the bottom line is impressive. In little more than one generation, hundreds of millions of people have risen from a life of day-to-day subsistence to a world of middle-class consumerism. Even those hundreds of millions who have not yet prospered—resentful though many may be—have the powerful example of their countrymen who have.

Not surprisingly, success has brought a new confidence among East Asian elites that they can hold their own with North America and Europe. In the mid-1990s, this self-confidence seemed to border on cultural arrogance as the region's politicians and intellectuals measured the "values" of Asia against those of the West and found them superior. Then, the financial crisis of the late nineties sapped their confidence in East Asia's "destiny," at least temporarily. In an international economy globalizing at a dizzying pace, there was no place to hide. Currencies plunged, banking systems imploded, unemployment shot up, and tens of millions slipped back below the poverty line. Fortunately, for most countries, growth resumed relatively quickly and self-confidence rose again soon after.

The big exception to the rebound has been Japan, where economic stagnation has lasted over a decade. Japanese diplomats and politicians watched in frustration as their country's position declined from "Number One" in the eighties. But Japan still remains the largest and most advanced economy in Asia by a big margin, and we found cautious confidence in Japan and elsewhere that the country has finally regained economic traction and is poised to resume sustained growth. For now and probably for the indefinite future, China has replaced Japan as the primary engine of East Asian growth. Yet as some things change, other things remain the same. The United States used to pound on Japan to open its markets and let its currency rise. In this new era, the United States beseeches China to revalue its currency. In both cases, the solutions to the American current account deficit mainly lie elsewhere—namely, at home.

East Asia's global economic weight has not yet been matched by increased international political influence, collectively or individually. With the important exception of Japan (and tiny Singapore), East Asian countries remain absorbed with domestic affairs. Few seek to strut on a world stage, and again, with the exception of Japan, they contribute little to international humanitarian enterprises or the activities of the United Nations. That being said, China has begun to reach out and engage multilaterally, even in UN peacekeeping. China's concerns about its exploding needs for energy and other raw materials have led to an active economic diplomacy in the Middle East, Africa, and Latin America. Beijing's economic growth and expanding global agenda has stirred the bureaucrats and think tankers in Washington.

Indeed, China is now invited in a serious way to help solve grave international problems such as nuclear weapons proliferation by North Korea and Iran.

In general, however, the countries of East Asia, including China, have a long way to go in acquiring the habits of constructive global involvement. Cultivating such habits will be necessary, however, if East Asia's global influence is to grow and eventually permit East Asia to lay claim to its own century to follow the American one. The "Asian century"—some would say the "Chinese century"—is likely only a matter of time, but it will probably not arrive all that quickly. China has yet to acquire moral force.

WHAT AMERICANS SEE

The United States, of course, has played an enormous part in the transformation of East Asia. During the cold war, Americans ran Japan for a time, helped create states in Taiwan and South Korea, fought two bloody wars, and brought millions of East Asians into our own population. We gave massive amounts of aid and technical assistance to friends and allies in the region. Huge expenditures in Asia during the Korean and Vietnam wars helped jumpstart growth in many East Asian countries. Highways in Thailand built by the U.S. military to connect American bases for bombing campaigns in Indochina opened up vast new tracts of territory for Thai agriculture and led to significantly expanded exports. We also furthered our own commercial interests. Capital and technology flowed westward across the Pacific, generating profits for U.S. companies, while inexpensive, increasingly high-quality manufactured goods flowed back to the United States.

Once the cold war ended, our preoccupation with the area diminished; at least that is how many in East Asia have seen it, and many, especially in Southeast Asia, still do. But history, national interest, and money keep drawing us back. Taiwan and North Korea continue to require our close attention. Our concerns about a possible global disaster led us to take the lead, albeit belatedly, to stem the Asian financial crisis of the late nineties. Above all, East Asia's dramatic economic growth is bringing American and East Asian economic destinies together in ways that would have been inconceivable just a decade ago. We are indeed in new territory; the question is whether we are responding in appropriate ways.

Two Disparate Areas

U.S. policy in East Asia has had to deal with two widely different areas, each with its own set of American interests and different problems. Northeast Asia has arguably become the most important area of the world for the United States, if not the center of American policy. Economic, political, and military power—actual and potential—resides there; our relations with Japan, South Korea, and Taiwan are among the closest in the world. Northeast Asia is where we station our military forces in the region. The thorniest security problems—the Taiwan Strait and North Korea—are there. Looming over all is the question of how China's integration into East Asia and the world turns out.

It strains credulity in 2006 to look back over four decades and recall that President Eisenhower riding to the inauguration in 1961 told John Kennedy that his biggest foreign policy problem would be Laos—the heart of Southeast Asia. Today, most Americans have probably only the vaguest sense of where Laos is. Southeast Asia is a mixed bag for American policy. Thailand, Singapore, and Malaysia have become dynamic, largely successful states. Indonesia and the Philippines are big states with considerable potential, but they have struggled, so far not very successfully, to deliver better governance and higher living standards to their people. Vietnam has gotten little attention from the United States—with perhaps the noted exception of the Pentagon—but has great economic promise and could be a stabilizing force in the area. Burma, Laos, and Cambodia are mired in poverty, and Burma is led by an internationally reviled government.

Southeast Asia also has East Asia's major regional cooperative structure, the Association of Southeast Asian Nations (ASEAN). Over the past forty years, ASEAN's members have grown to ten (Thailand, Indonesia, Malaysia, the Philippines, Singapore, Brunei, Vietnam, Burma, Laos, and Cambodia), and they have stayed together but have had trouble developing and implementing a common agenda that rises above generalities. While the United States does not ignore ASEAN—it certainly gives it plenty of lip service—it is not an anchor point for American policy. Instead, U.S. policymakers continue to focus bilaterally on the nations most important to American interests.

Since the end of the cold war, the United States seems to get involved in Southeast Asia only when there is trouble—the financial crisis of 1997 and the disastrous tsunami in 2004 come to mind. Whatever the United States does, Southeast Asians complain incessantly about our lack of attention, even though it is hard to figure out what they would have the United States do differently. We put this question to numerous interlocutors in the area and usually received rather vague recommendations to "pay more attention" or "to take ASEAN more seriously" or "to stop focusing only on terrorism." For some it was just the idea of the United States "being there." America's limited involvement in Southeast Asia, if that is what it is, may be simply because from the U.S. point of view the situation there has been broadly satisfactory, or at least not greatly threatening to our interests.

September 11, however, led the United States to pay attention to jihadism in the region, particularly in Indonesia and the Philippines, where pockets of violence had festered. Washington now works with most governments in the area to improve their counterterrorism capabilities, promote civil society, and reinforce the generally secular and tolerant leanings of Muslims in the region. It is not likely to be a short-term concern.

China's growing economic and political influence in Southeast Asia has drawn more and more American attention. The extent to which this is threatening to our interests is not all that apparent. In any event, we doubt that much can be done to reverse this trend, even if Southeast Asians really would want it reversed, given the great benefits China's growth is bringing to the region. Southeast Asian nations are prepared to live with a larger, more intrusive Chinese presence. As one senior Malaysian figure told us: "For what it's worth, we will not kowtow to China, but we will be deferential." Perhaps he meant they will bow from the waist but not from the knees. However, many in the region still say they would like to see a more active, more attentive United States as something of a "counterbalance" to China.

CHINA "AS NUMBER ONE," AT LEAST IN EAST ASIA

The "rise of China" has become a massive cliché. Great quantities of ink have been spent analyzing what this "rise" implies for the rest of Asia, for the United States, and for the world. It is, of course, a world-transforming development. The pecking order of regional power—economic, political, and military—is undergoing radical change. Despite the immense problems of poverty, growing disparities of wealth, and the difficulties of maintaining central control, "China shakes the world," to quote the prescient title journalist Jack Belden gave his book over fifty years ago.

While China's economic growth has vast positive implications for all of East Asia, many observers, inside and outside the region, worry that in addition to shaking the world, China is slowly assuming a twenty-first century version of its traditional imperial political role in East Asia. Indeed, the road to Beijing is increasingly well traveled. It has been some two hundred years since the world has had any experience with a powerful China. Nor, as Singapore's Minister Mentor Lee Kuan Yew first famously observed, has the world ever seen a strong China and a strong Japan at the same time.

The Chinese themselves—even at top levels—have debated the implications of the word "rise," although these days they seem to prefer "peaceful development." Some Chinese officials like to tell visitors they have pursued this inquiry in search of lessons to be learned, so that China can go right, where past rising powers like pre–World War I Germany went wrong. Other Chinese officials are less reluctant to express pride in China's growing power and assumption of its rightful place toward the head of the table. To date, China's leadership has been generally prudent and patient, intent on not antagonizing major economic partners, particularly the United States. They also do not want to arouse the neighborhood, although when it comes to Japan, they seem to take glee in sticking in the knife, as they did to Japan's bid in 2005 for a permanent UN Security Council seat. The Chinese leadership, like the American one, also has to straddle two centuries.

The discussion in the United States on China's rise has been a debate between optimists and pessimists over China's internal dynamics and international aspirations. Some believe that China's economic dynamism will continue, that prosperity will spread inland from the coast, that the "communist" regime, whatever its perturbations, will gradually open more political space, and that enlightened self-interest and pressures from a bourgeoning middle class will constrain China's exercise of pressure and leverage. Similarly, for the optimists the essential domestic political requirement for rapid economic growth for decades to come and the dependence on foreign trade should help keep China on a constructive nonthreatening course in its international dealings.

Other close observers of China see a country beset by smoldering social and economic tensions, particularly in the countryside, and enormous environmental difficulties that will ultimately result in political or economic breakdown or both, including the end of the Communist Party, or produce a nationalistic spasm that threatens peace in the region. The pessimists often argue that the authoritarian and ostensibly communist government no longer has any vision, no moral authority, that economic growth alone is not enough to sustain the party's rule, and that the regime will not be able to manage future leadership transitions and both stability and growth will come crashing down. Some experts have been predicting political and economic breakdown for years; one day, they may be right.

Debate also is intense over whether a China ruled by a secretive and authoritarian Communist Party is predestined to pursue policies that will threaten American interests in East Asia and globally. For some Americans it is almost an article of faith, or at least an historical deduction, that China as a rising power will inevitably want to spread its wings, that its currently benign posture is a transitional one, and that as the country continues to gain weight and strength it will assert itself in an increasingly aggressive way. Over time, they believe, economic power will translate into expanded military capability, and China will challenge American influence in areas of its choosing not only economically but also militarily. Not surprisingly, a great deal of vagueness as to where, when, and why usually accompanies such assertions. More tangible concerns abound in American defense circles regarding Taiwan. The fear is that deterrence will fray, and the United States would not be able to dominate the Taiwan Strait without serious losses should hostilities erupt. There are similar worries that if the regime came under serious internal stress, its leaders would fall back on nationalism and xenophobia to help them survive. Taiwan and Japan would be the obvious foils.

The Bush administration early on identified China as its principal strategic challenge. September 11 diverted American attention and defused a potentially fierce China debate in Washington. The tenor of our relations radically changed as we sought cooperation from China on counterterrorism and the elimination of North Korea's nuclear weapons programs. Beijing saw this as an opportunity and responded in a constructive manner. Given the American public's negative image of China's government and growing perceptions as well as great congressional clamor that China threatens American economic well being, the pendulum could swing back as it has done before in our relations. Both the left and the right focus their ire on China—on democracy and human rights; on the trade deficit, the theft of intellectual property, the loss of manufacturing jobs, and the undervalued currency; and increasingly, on China's potential military threat. The list grows longer, and our politicians have ample opportunity to rail against China. Nevertheless, President Bush has proceeded more pragmatically than even many of his champions would prefer, and he has tried hard to keep relations with Beijing on a steady and constructive course.

Whatever American defense concerns, East Asia (indeed, all countries) has a growing stake in China's continued economic success. Economic interdependence is already such that a so-called hard landing for the Chinese economy would have a devastating effect. Everyone has his or her own pick on the outcome of this global horse race, but the fact is that there is not much agreement in the United States on how we should deal with the new China. Without more of a consensus on this issue, our ability to relate effectively to the "new" East Asia will be difficult.

JAPAN AND CHINA—EAST ASIA'S ODD COUPLE

Japan may be coming to view China's military intentions with less equanimity than the authors do. In the past few years, relations between the two have worsened significantly. The history of the first half of the twentieth century remains an open sore in Northeast Asia and a stick that China, as well as the two Koreas, waves menacingly over Japanese heads. (China, of course, publicly ignores much of its own contemporary history and the massive misdeeds of the Chinese Communist Party in China and elsewhere in Asia.) China and Japan also quarrel about claims to various Pacific islands and the surrounding waters where there may be oil and gas deposits. Neither country's leadership presently seems able to talk constructively to the other about how to address the past, much less how to heal their differences and pursue obvious common interests in East Asia's prosperity and stability. At bottom China seems to regard Japan as part of the West and a lackey of the Americans. There is a corresponding and growing Japanese tendency toward skepticism, even hostility, regarding the Chinese political system, its lack of democratic practice and political values in general.

Beijing is unhappy with the trends of Japanese defense policy of the past few years. It sees Japan shedding its post–World War II inhibitions on the size and capabilities of its Self-Defense Forces and redefining their role and mission in the region. Beijing perceives that Japan is prodding the United States to join an anti-China alliance or is a willing partner in the American effort to contain China. For its part, Japan is now the fourth largest defense spender in the world and clearly measures its own capabilities against those of China. It has moved its forces from north to south, no longer fearful of an attack by Russia. The public perception of a hostile threat from a nuclear-capable North Korea armed with ballistic missiles reinforces those elements in Japan pressing for a more muscular national security posture. Some Japanese, perhaps even a majority, long to be a "normal" country, that is, to reduce the constitutional constraints on Japan's national security policy and eventually develop a greater capability to project force in the region.

The Chinese assessment of general defense trends in Japan is realistic, but their concerns for the future seem largely excessive. Despite some rise in nationalism, the Japanese public is still pacifist and conciliatory. They remain quite comfortable in the strategic embrace of the American alliance and are generally opposed to acquiring nuclear weapons, one of the benefits of the U.S.-Japan alliance.

East Asia's future will depend heavily on how relations between these two giants evolve. If anything would stimulate Japan militarily, it is likely to be a major expansion in China's naval capabilities, which would generate fears about the security of its sea lanes. At the moment, the U.S. government approach to the Chinese-Japanese relationship is to view Japan as an essential, long-term ally and quietly encourage dialogue and restraint on both sides. But some in national security policy circles, particularly on the Republican right, really prefer an explicit alliance against China, and the present Defense Department seems inclined in that direction.

COLD WAR PERENNIALS

Focusing on longer-term considerations is difficult when the United States remains preoccupied with the difficult, dangerous, and costly problems of the Taiwan Strait and North Korea. These two hot spots developed long ago under different historical circumstances. The United States and most of its friends continue to see America's involvement as essential to preventing war in both cases and a basic test of American credibility.

Taiwan. Taiwan is China's "renegade province," and Beijing sees a democratic Taiwan as a direct threat to its national unity and the future of the Communist Party. It fears that Taiwan's government will pursue independence as a political rallying call. This concern resonates widely in China, even among the proponents of greater openness and political reform.

The United States is dedicated to preserving the peace in the Taiwan Strait and maintains forces to deter conflict. It pursues a delicately balanced strategy: reassuring or chastising Taiwan as the situation requires—including warnings and admonitions by the president himself when Taiwan leaders make statements that raise Beijing's hackles. At the same time, the United States keeps China at bay by constant reassurances about its dedication to a One China policy, carefully calibrated threats as needed, and occasional displays of power in the Taiwan area. Most Americans probably believe democratic Taiwan deserves independence, but they show little interest in going to war to help Taiwan to get it. Indeed, according to a 2005 Gallup poll, the majority of Americans believe Taiwan and China are already two separate, sovereign states.

And so the United States continues to deal with the Taiwan issue by exporting it to the future, as it has done successfully for half a century. Giving "Chinese pragmatism" time to work its magic has not brought a resolution, nor has Taiwan's increasing economic integration into China gone anywhere politically. No one has come up with salable policy alternatives, but the hope is still that in time something will turn up. The prevalent view is not to disturb a dangerous but reasonably stable situation.

North Korea. North Korea is the world's only monolithic hereditary dictatorship—as odious a state as there is. It still has the capability to inflict enormous death and destruction on South Korea. North Korea is pursuing—indeed likely has achieved—the production of nuclear weapons and delivery systems. While the fear of a North Korean conventional attack on South Korea has receded, the United States has a treaty commitment to defend the South and must be prepared to do so.

The current North Korean nuclear issue seems like the remake of a bad movie. We saw the original version in 1994, when the United States worked out an agreement with North Korea to stop its plutonium production program. It fell apart eight years later. The remake has a more numerous and complicated cast than the original and will hopefully have a better ending, though that is far from assured. One unfortunate side effect of the reemergence of a nuclear crisis has been a weakening of the U.S. alliance with South Korea as our two governments have distinctly different approaches to dealing with Pyongyang. But reality can intrude on ideology and policy, and after three years of stonewalling, the Bush administration now may be prepared to reinvent the same sort of agreement that the United States concluded in 1994, though it is likely to be more expensive this time around. It is not clear that a deal can be struck—even if the parties are serious— and that could bring about a huge crisis as early as 2006.

Indeed, periodic crises have punctuated both cold war holdovers, and both defy simple solutions. Neither can be peacefully managed— to say nothing of peacefully resolved—without American involvement. And that may not be enough. Miscalculation and miscommunication could produce horrible results.

THE NEW REGIONALISM

Just as large flows of direct investment from both inside and outside East Asia have powered economic growth, so have they brought its economies closer together with rapid increases in intraregional trade and investment, freer movement of people across borders, and, perhaps most important, development of an Asian middle class. There is also a growing recognition that integration of economies produces vulnerabilities as well as opportunities. The rapid spread of financial panic in the late nineties was a wake-up call. Despite nationalistic tensions and bilateral economic differences in this diverse region, governments have become more willing to talk seriously, if still discordantly, about closer East Asian cooperation, including the construction of new regional institutions.

The late nineties brought the relatively rapid emergence of a new regional grouping—ASEAN Plus Three (Japan, China, and South Korea)—focused on trade and financial cooperation. (This grouping largely mirrors our definition of East Asia.) Since 2001 there has been growing talk of enhancing East Asian Community building. A concrete step, perhaps, was the holding of an East Asian Summit (EAS) in Kuala Lumpur in December 2005. Somewhere down the pike may lie an East Asian Community (EAC), obviously far different than the European model but potentially important in its own right. Right now, such a community, even with a small "c," is mostly still a vision, one however that is grabbing the attention of the region.

Rhetoric has generally outdistanced performance in East Asia's efforts at regional cooperation over the past few decades. Today, however, actual integration is the expanding reality, and it is galvanizing governments. Unlike the early stages of European integration, economics—not politics—has been the driving force and creates an immediate substance for cooperation.

East Asia's growing regionalism reflects more than an interest in managing the consequences of economic integration. Deepening regional cooperation is seen by many countries as a potentially important political tool to help prevent conflict in the area and particularly "to domesticate" China. Its proponents would like to tie China into a web of reciprocal obligations and benefits that they believe will enhance China's self-interest in using its new power prudently and taking fuller account of its neighbors' interests. China seems to have confidence that, given its growing strength, some restraint on its freedom of action may be an acceptable price for reassuring the neighborhood that its growing strength is not threatening. A few countries also see regional integration as a way of reducing American influence.

Wider and deeper regional cooperation in East Asia will face many obstacles starting with the basic disparate nature of the region. It is ironic that the two big powers in East Asia are simultaneously quarreling with one another and urging greater East Asian institutionalized cooperation. Unless Sino-Japanese antagonism abates, greater East Asian regional cooperation will not gain much lift.

THE AMERICAN DILEMMA—HOW TO STRADDLE TWO CENTURIES

THE AMERICAN SILHOUETTE

The American foundation in East Asia remains strong. The power of the American market and the reach of American financial institutions are enormous. American popular culture is pervasive, although alternatives are emerging in the region. American higher education remains a highly valued commodity, although here too new options are appearing. Political elites still respect American power and determination—and American values—even if they frequently disagree with our policies.

Asians above all have wanted continuity and constancy in U.S. policy. In our experience over the years, they prefer Republicans to Democrats because they believe Republicans have been firmer on critical security issues. On the other hand, popular antipathy to the Bush administration may be pushing East Asians away from a preference for the elephant over the donkey. East Asian elites tend to see the United States currently as dangerously self-absorbed and somewhat separated from reality.

Both China and Japan assume that America's interest and deep involvement in East Asia will continue. They may fret about the lack of policy continuity between administrations, but no one thinks we are about to go away, even though many Americans think that is China's goal. One senior Chinese foreign ministry official answered metaphorically when we asked how failure in Iraq would affect attitudes in China about American "reliability." He laughed and said, "We think of you Americans as great surgeons going around the world performing remarkable surgeries but then you move on to open up the next patient before you sew up the last one. We think you made a mistake going into Iraq. But you remain the most powerful country in the world, and your interests in East Asia are too great for you to walk away from." He did not add that China is not exactly dismayed to see the United States tied down in Iraq.

One might have assumed that the escalating power of China would cause countries in the region to value our presence more highly, and many do, especially in Southeast Asia. But they tend increasingly to say this sotto voce. The Chinese are probably listening, and few want to offend Beijing. Even Lee Kwan Yew, always free with advice, has lowered his public voice about the importance of America's involvement in the region's security and talks more about the inevitability of China's economic advance, seemingly accepting that the U.S. presence is bound to shrink relative to China's. It is worth noting that ASEAN, setting the criteria for participation, found a diplomatic formula that would prevent the United States from attending the first EAS. (See Chapter 2.)

Only Japan has moved to enhance its alliance with the United States. Tokyo has not hesitated to endorse the wider use of our forces based in Japan in the region and beyond and move its own forces beyond the East Asian region. As further evidence of support for the United States, as well as its own interests and its problems with China, only Japan has publicly indicated, very noticeably in February 2005, its concern over the security of Taiwan, importantly in a joint statement with the United States.

One of the less noticed trends in East Asia is the emergence of a new generation of nationalist leaders, particularly in democratic countries, who are no longer willing to accept the delivered wisdom of the United States—one of the unintended consequences of democracy promotion. In South Korea, for example, the generations born after the Korean War, including many current politicians and government officials, are reexamining their history and claiming to see a self-serving American hand that propped up authoritarian military leaders. Indeed, the present South Korean government even seems at times determined to revise Korea's past. They are increasingly attentive to China, which has supplanted the United States as South Korea's largest trading partner and whose views regarding North Korea are, at least for the immediate future, more compatible with their own than are those of the United States. The U.S.–South Korean military alliance—although still firm—no longer seems an assured long-term element in East Asia's future.

U.S. credibility among Asian publics has plummeted in recent years, but negative attitudes toward America existed well before George W. Bush came to office. Young people in particular, from Indonesia to China, are highly critical of the United States even as they work hard to get here for education or employment. Chinese students cannot be budged from an angry belief that the bombing of the Chinese Embassy in Belgrade in 1999 was deliberate. Few in East Asia support American efforts in Iraq, and those countries, like South Korea and Japan who have sent troops, did so as an investment in their alliances with the United States, not because they agree with the policy. Among East Asia's Muslim population there is a strident antagonism toward American policies on Iraq and the Arab-Israeli issue. The longevity of these attitudes remains to be seen. Events have a way of altering perceptions—for good or for ill. The American humanitarian response to the December 2004 Indian Ocean tsunami and Pakistan's earthquake in October 2005 restored some measure of goodwill in the area, at least temporarily.

We found that America's "soft power"—historically invaluable if not as visible as its "hard power"—is declining. For one thing, we have more rivals in the soft power competition. East Asia is developing a vibrant contemporary culture that offers alternatives to Hollywood and MTV. In television and film, South Korea, Hong Kong, and others are now producing for all of East Asia, not just for local markets. In higher education, it is not only post–September 11 difficulty in obtaining student visas that has reduced the number of East Asian applicants to American universities. There are newly credible alternatives. The region, particularly China, is investing heavily in homegrown alternatives to Harvard, Stanford, Oxford, and Cambridge. While these institutions have a long way to go to match the depth and breadth of their Western models, they are making progress, and they are far less expensive than their American rivals. Fluency in English will continue to be an essential tool for success internationally, but younger East Asians increasingly see fluency in Mandarin as a marketable skill.

Does this shift in attitudes and perceptions have serious policy significance? We believe it does. It limits bilateral cooperation in Muslim countries and our ability to mobilize support in the United Nations and other international institutions. It constrains government policies that otherwise could be more accommodating to U.S. policy. Over the longer term, growing negativism toward the United States can corrode our interests—and lessen our influence. New governments will come to power as in South Korea that are less bound by history and less in awe of the United States. This concern about how others see us is mirrored in increasing American self-criticism over the

U.S. government's failure to win support for its policies and calls for a more effective "public diplomacy." The problem, of course, often lies with the policies themselves.

If the United States has begun to lose some degree of influence in East Asia—and we find that it has—we can take some consolation that the decline results from our successes as well as our failures. While the cost of our efforts has been great in blood and monies, the United States has achieved a large measure of its original postwar aims in East Asia: growth, stability, democracy, and independence. Unfortunately, however, as a former Turkish president once proclaimed: "Yesterday was yesterday, today is today."

MANAGING IN A NEW EAST ASIA

Enhancing our moral and political position in East Asia is an important task, but it is hardly the whole story. We have critically important policy issues to face.

The United States remains an incredibly dynamic country and a central player in the region. But it is having difficulty getting used to a new East Asia where American power is still great but its sway much less. That could get worse. Japan was and still is a competitive challenge, but it has been largely an American follower in geopolitical terms. Now we have a 600 pound gorilla in the neighborhood, perhaps going on 800 pounds. It is definitely not a poodle, and we fulminate about China even as we devour its goods and vie to get into its markets. Just stop at Wal-Mart or Marks & Spencer. Even South Korea, a smaller but impressive dynamo, no longer marches to our tune on critical matters, while much of Southeast Asia is enthralled by or, like Burma and Cambodia, beholden to China.

We also have developed new dependencies. Our interest rates and capital markets are dependent on the willingness of East Asian central banks to hold enormous amounts of American debt generated by ballooning trade deficits. Our homeland security depends on the cooperation of Indonesia, Thailand, and others in exchanging intelligence and undertaking joint police action against terrorists. Our companies and workers are vulnerable to rapidly shifting patterns of comparative advantage as Asia moves up the technological ladder. We must adjust to higher prices for commodities, notably energy, as East Asia's demand surges. While the benefits to the United States of

East Asia's success far outweigh the costs, that is not always or even usually evident in our domestic political discourse.

Meanwhile, the United States has to be constantly attentive to the two issues carried over from the last century—Taiwan and North Korea—where the burden of deterrence is significantly ours. We devote great time and major financial and human resources to these problems. We are comfortable with this because it plays to America's one undisputed strength—its military power—and monies are readily available. But this creates a tendency to view the new East Asia from a largely military perspective, especially when it comes to China. The reality is that the utility of military force, beyond the Taiwan and North Korean issues, is not all that compelling to many East Asian countries as they consider how to balance the nature of their long-term relationship with China and their equities with the United States. It is similarly questionable whether military power remains all that relevant to our desire to guard access to resources and markets in East Asia, or even to our traditional concerns over keeping open the principal sea lanes through the region.

The challenge for the United States in this region in this new century seems increasingly one of managing globalization and economic competition—the drive for markets, the growth of new technologies, and the critical requirement for human talent. In the long run, what East Asia offers the world is not just inexpensive labor, but impressive intellectual power and enormously hardworking and market-oriented peoples as well. The competitive challenge promises to be increasingly formidable. Our own chances for success in that competition will not be enhanced by simply providing more resources for our military. Such a one-dimensional approach to the region will stir the competitive juices of our potential rivals and discomfit our friends and allies. The increasing economic and perhaps political integration of East Asia will strengthen both these reactions.

The American relationship with the new East Asia will be determined in large part by four interrelated big issues:

◆   The way we deal with China's emergence as a great player on the international scene. Will we try to balance an economic/political approach with a heavy military containment effort? If so, how? Do we try to get China to be a responsible "stakeholder" in the

international system, as Deputy Secretary of State Robert
Zoellick urged in his frequently cited speech on China in
September 2005, drawing them into helping us manage the international system much as we have over the past several decades?
Or do we accept that life may be a little different and that stake-
holders, especially ones on the rise, may want a substantial role
in setting the course and not just following it?

◆   Effective handling of the Taiwan and North Korean issues is crit-
    ical to continued peace in East Asia. These two potential flash-
    points are an inescapable part of managing U.S. relations with
    China, Japan, and South Korea as well as the wider global issue
    of nonproliferation. Our skill in dealing with these issues remains
    a major determinant of our ability to exercise leadership and
    influence in the region.

◆   A third issue is how we deal with Sino-Japanese competition.
    Some want to maintain a more vigorous military U.S.-Japan
    alliance directed against China. Others see this as geopolitical
    folly and argue that our efforts should focus on working seri-
    ously to reduce tensions between the two, getting Japan to come
    to terms more effectively with its past so it can play a more effec-
    tive role in the region.

◆   Lastly, how should Washington respond to efforts to build wider
    and more effective political and economic cooperation within
    East Asia? It is unclear at this point where that effort, including
    the notion of an East Asian Community, might go, but it will
    definitely not fade away. Its success (or failure) could have great
    impact on stability and growth in the region. The United States
    can influence—though not necessarily determine—the outcome
    of this effort. But first we will have to decide what outcome we
    want.

The chapters that follow discuss the key elements of these basic issues
in greater detail. We leave our own prescriptions to the last chapter,
to make it easier for impatient readers to skip to the end of the book
and see what our bottom lines are.

2

REGIONALISM
CHINA, EAST ASIA'S COMMUNITY BUILDER?

*E*ast Asian regionalism—the effort to build institutions to foster regional cooperation—has often made our eyes glaze over. So many meetings, so many top officials using high flown rhetoric, so many "wise men" feeding a cottage industry about the achievements of the Association of Southeast Asian Nations (ASEAN), the Asia-Pacific Economic Cooperation Forum (APEC), and the ASEAN Regional Forum (ARF)—and so little concrete action. Perhaps we have grown wiser over time, but we now believe that regionalism in East Asia is becoming a much more salient phenomenon with great consequences for the region and for the United States.

When we began working on this book with a trip to Northeast Asia in the late summer of 2004, one of the more striking phrases we heard from our Asian interlocutors was "East Asian community building." In Japan, a senior foreign ministry official characterized this project, including the convening of an East Asian Summit (EAS), as Japan's leading foreign policy undertaking for the coming years. His ministry inundated us with paper—wise men's reports, vision statements, and ministerial speeches.

All this came as something of a surprise to us. At that point, we had heard hardly a peep in Washington, except in a few academic circles and from low-level American diplomats, about the creation of an East Asian Community (EAC), and here in Asia high-level government officials were putting it at the top of their foreign policy priorities. In conversations on this trip and on our later visits to the rest of the region, we heard a lot more about the need to enhance ASEAN, to build new regional institutions, and eventually to create an EAC. Expanded regionalism seemed almost a mantra to explain how the nations of East Asia could better manage the vulnerabilities of economic interdependence; overcome historical animosities; defuse territorial disputes; address transnational problems, such as yellow dust, SARS, and bird flu; and even help bridge the gaps in governance and development within the region.

So where does all this talk come from, where is it going, and what does it mean for the United States?

First, we conclude it is more than just a subject of fashionable discourse among senior officials, academics, and politicians. In some respects, the current focus on community building follows from what has been happening in East Asia for some time—"the facts on the ground driving government policy," as an astute Japanese diplomat described it to us. East Asian regionalism has its roots in the vast changes in the economies of the region and the rapid growth of interdependence among them. East Asia's officials and business leaders are talking about the region in a new way, as an emerging area of deeply shared interests that needs to acquire the cohesion of common purpose it has never had. There seems to be a genuine interest—despite the animosities of the past and the spasms of present day nationalism—in examining this notion and hopefully building on it. There is one central reason for this new perspective, the extraordinary changes in the way the region works, in its politics, and in its thinking—all of which flow from China's dramatic transformation.

Much of the story of the global economy over the past several decades has been an East Asian story: its vast growth of output and trade that has fueled an unprecedented rise in living standards not only in East Asia, but in much of the rest of the world as well. But in recent years, the story of East Asia—and especially the story of economic integration—is more and more the story of China and the effects of its spectacular growth on the entire region. The manner of China's rise—its decision to open its economy to the outside world and invite massive inflows of foreign private investment—has produced a dramatic increase in connectedness among East Asia's economies. Integrated production networks crisscross national borders, producing trade and investment flows that knit the region together.

Greater connectedness also brings greater dependency and new vulnerabilities as the Asian financial crisis of the late nineties demonstrated, when financial weakness in Thailand spilled over into the rest of Southeast Asia and then north to Korea with devastating consequences. One consequence of the financial crisis was a loss of confidence in U.S.-led international institutions, such as the International Monetary Fund (IMF), and a new focus on the need for regional institutions to defend against future financial trauma. China's growing ties to all the countries of the region also has brought a realignment of power relationships within the region, which in turn produces new anxieties. Many in East Asia have concluded that coping with these anxieties is best done within a framework of regional institutions.

It is too early to do much more than speculate about the eventual results of East Asia's new focus on regional cooperation. Some think it is all Asian palaver, a replay of some of the overblown rhetoric of years past about ASEAN and its achievements. Indeed, the obstacles to East Asian community building are formidable, starting with the vast differences in the nature of the individual states. Recently, the governments of China and Japan have been barely able to speak to one another, much less collaborate in building regional cooperation. Most governments of Southeast Asia remain preoccupied with domestic issues and have limited human resources and energy for concrete regional undertakings. Moreover, while the potential virtues of an EAC may be considerable, countries are far from a consensus on what it would actually do and who would participate. Another new regional institution—the East Asian Summit (EAS)—was a subject of intense jockeying and debate over the invitation list, the agenda, and its possible relationship to East Asian community building efforts. In its first meeting, the EAS produced little of substance other than to decide to meet again in 2006. It was mostly important as a happening.

However serious the obstacles, East Asia's continued economic success is increasingly hostage to the ability of the region's governments not just to get along with one another but also to collaborate effectively on common issues and problems—from enormous environmental degradation to communicable diseases. Even the continued growth of trade and investment will require greater government-to-government cooperation.

What does this all mean for the United States? For the most part, the United States still looks at East Asia primarily through a bilateral prism. American officials, however, have not been able to ignore current East Asian efforts to forge more regional cooperation. There is irritation and concern in Washington that many East Asian governments presently seem to envision an EAC that would not include the United States—even going so far as to organize an EAS meeting without inviting the American president. So far, the U.S. government has taken a low posture, content to praise the proliferation of new multilateral regional initiatives. As things stand now, the United States is nowhere near the center of East Asian efforts to build new regional institutions. We seem to have a wait and see policy. When all is said and done, what probably bothers Americans most about the direction of East Asian regionalism is not so much that the countries have the audacity to organize themselves without the active engagement of the United States. The burr under the American saddle is the China factor and the possibility that new regional institutions will somehow consolidate China's growing stature within East Asia at America's expense.

THE TIES THAT BIND

East Asian governments are trying hard to catch up politically with growing economic interdependence. If measured simply in terms of trade, integration has grown enormously. In 1981, intra-Asian trade accounted for 33 percent of the region's global trade. By 2001, that percentage had risen to 45 percent, and, by 2004, it was at 49 percent. Feverish activity is going on in many countries below the radar screen of outside governments.

Foreign direct investment from within the region as well as from outside has been a critical element of both growth and economic integration. East Asian companies, especially from Japan and South Korea, are moving production facilities into China and Southeast Asia. Western multinationals invest throughout East Asia not just to produce for export back to North America and Western Europe as was the case a decade ago, but increasingly to sell into exploding East Asian markets for consumer goods and capital equipment. While many argue that East Asia is still too wedded to export-led economic growth, domestic investment and consumption are becoming much more important components of that economic growth.

Economic integration in East Asia has been largely a private sector phenomenon driven by market forces, not government planning. In Europe the creation of a single market and a single currency were the product of some fifty years of governments setting goals and timetables and aligning legal and regulatory norms. East Asian governments are only now trying to build political cooperation on the base of the considerable economic interdependence that already exists. The question of what might be a desirable, realistic end result for these new aspirations has barely been raised. As one of our Indonesian friends put it, "Asians are assembling what goes into the box before they try to design the box itself."

We are not witnessing the creation of an inward looking regional trading bloc. Far from it. Even as regional interdependence grows, East Asian economies also are becoming even more integrated into the global economy. Intra-Asian trade numbers tend to understate the significance of the region's dependence on global markets. For example, only half of East Asia's exports within the region reflect final demand; the other half consists of components and semi-manufactured goods moving within regional supply chains and eventually sold outside the region. A large share of the intra-Asian trade also is carried out by Western corporations that are invested in the region. Moreover, almost 60 percent of China's exports to the United States are produced by foreign firms, many of them American firms with divisions in China. Thus, East Asia remains dependent—some argue much too dependent—on international capital markets and inflows of Western technology.

An earlier phase of East Asian regionalization was fueled by high levels of Japanese development assistance and foreign direct investment in the seventies and eighties. Japanese exports of capital goods to the rest of East Asia produced exports back to Japan of both components and finished products for sale in Japan or re-export. But Japan's role as an integrating force in East Asia waned in the early nineties, as its economy went into protracted stagnation and its companies cut back investment everywhere, including East Asia. The share of exports to Japan from the rest of East Asia declined from 25 percent in 1981, to 14 percent in 2001.

Over the past decade, China has replaced Japan as the engine of East Asian economic regionalization. Since the early eighties, China's seemingly inexhaustible pools of disciplined, inexpensive labor have attracted foreign investment. Those workers are now becoming consumers, and major international companies have concluded that they must have a presence in China and elsewhere in Asia with close proximity to China, not only to be competitive globally but also to be able to sell in East Asia itself if they are going to have a coherent global business strategy. The net effect is that more and more capital, raw materials, component parts, finished products, and people cross national borders as integrated parts of the same production networks.

China's industrial advance also has a strong competitive impact on its neighbors, forcing them (and the United States too) to undertake the often painful process of financial restructuring and economic rationalization to find a place in the shifting regional mix of comparative advantage. At the same time, the size and rapid growth of the China market has made it a primary outlet for exports from other East Asian countries. The numbers are telling. (See Table 2.1.) For example, China has become South Korea's largest export market, Japan's trade with China now exceeds its trade with the United States, and China is now the first or second trading partner for almost every country in East Asia. East Asia's countries also have increased their share of China's imports from 15 percent in 1980 to nearly 53 percent in 2003. (See Table 2.2.)

The interconnectedness between the peoples of East Asia also is growing. A rapidly expanding, consumption-minded, urban middle class is acquiring new habits and behavior, similar to the middle-class ways of Americans and Europeans. These modern Asians are less and less concerned about the national origin of the goods they buy. Price and quality are what is important. Middle-class Asians are on the Internet, comparison shopping for automobiles and furniture for their new condominiums. They have become as deeply concerned with the education of their children as the Japanese have been. And they are fomenting a new, still fragile, sense of community that is further bringing East Asia together.

The rapid growth of intra-Asian tourism is another new force drawing the region closer together. Japanese tourists have long been found everywhere. Nowadays Chinese tourists are just as omnipresent. Municipal governments in South Korea are building

TABLE 2.1. EXPORTS OF SELECTED ECONOMIES TO CHINA
(AS PERCENT OF TOTAL EXPORTS)

	1980	1985	1990	1995	2000	2002	2003
Japan	3.9	7.1	2.1	5.0	6.3	9.6	13.6
South Korea	0.0	0.0	0.0	7.0	10.7	14.7	20.5
Hong Kong SAR	6.3	26.0	24.8	33.3	34.5	39.3	42.7
Singapore	1.6	1.5	1.5	2.3	3.9	5.5	7.0
Indonesia	0.0	0.5	3.2	3.8	4.5	5.1	7.4
Malaysia	1.7	1.0	2.1	2.6	3.1	5.6	10.8
Philippines	0.8	1.8	0.8	1.2	1.7	3.9	12.0
Thailand	1.9	3.8	1.2	2.9	4.1	5.2	7.1
India	0.3	0.3	0.1	0.9	1.8	4.2	6.4
European Union	0.8	1.8	1.2	2.2	2.7	3.4	4.2
United States	1.7	1.8	1.2	2.0	2.1	3.2	3.9
Germany	0.6	1.2	0.6	1.5	1.6	2.2	2.6

Source: Eswar Prasad, ed., *China's Growth and Integration into the World Economy: Prospects and Challenges* (Washington, D.C.: International Monetary Fund, 2004), p. 8, available online at http://www.imf.org/external/pubs/ft/op/232/op232.pdf.

TABLE 2.2. CHINA'S SOURCES OF IMPORTS
(AS PERCENT OF TOTAL IMPORTS)

	1980	1990	1995	2000	2002	2003
Asia	15.0	41.0	47.1	53.5	53.1	52.8
ASEAN	3.4	5.6	7.4	9.3	10.4	11.3
Japan	26.5	14.2	21.9	17.8	18.1	18.0
South Korea	—	0.4	7.8	10.0	9.7	10.4
Taiwan	—	—	11.2	11.3	12.9	12.9
European Union	15.8	17.0	16.1	13.3	13.1	12.9
United States	19.6	12.2	12.2	9.6	9.2	8.2

Source: Eswar Prasad, ed., *China's Growth and Integration into the World Economy: Prospects and Challenges* (Washington, D.C.: International Monetary Fund, 2004), p. 6, available online at http://www.imf.org/external/pubs/ft/op/232/op232.pdf.

new facilities to attract Chinese tourists. Chinese, Japanese, and Koreans are going on golfing holidays all over Southeast Asia. Food malls from Seoul to Manila and Hong Kong to Kuala Lumpur now offer a full range of Asian cuisines as well as the ubiquitous hamburgers and pizza. Film and music exports within the area are booming, and Japanese housewives schedule their days around the latest Korean TV soap opera.

East Asians are also leaving their own countries to work in other East Asian countries. They are not just maids from the Philippines in Hong Kong and Singapore, but skilled workers, managers, and entrepreneurs from almost every country in the region. Young professionals are learning Mandarin and flocking to universities in China. These newly urbanized, more affluent Asians still consider themselves Chinese, Japanese, Korean, and so forth, but they also have begun to think of themselves as Asian in ways that their parents and grandparents never did. As they become better educated and more knowledgeable about the world, they are developing some common expectations about business practices, the performance of governments, and the role of civil society. This expanding, educated middle class is likely to be a force in the building of any EAC. All this is promising, but one must not exaggerate. National identities still count most.

The trend toward a greater East Asian consciousness, self-awareness, and confidence would be hard to stop, even if someone wanted to. Importantly, however, for the United States and the rest of the world, this is not becoming a phenomenon of isolation and exclusion. East Asians need and want to be a part of the so-called global community, and their aspirations are increasingly international in thought and action.

Whatever the implications of continuing East Asian economic integration for the United States and its posture and influence in the region, America will remain an immensely powerful economic player in the region. American-based companies are a primary source of foreign direct investment, even while East Asian central banks accumulate enormous holdings of American dollars. Our capital markets determine in large measure how much Asian companies pay for capital, at least those not enjoying governmental subsidies. And continued access to the American market is vital to China and other East Asian producers of consumer goods and capital equipment.

AN EMERGING EAST ASIAN COMMUNITY?

East Asia—Northeast and Southeast—is not a coherent area geographically, ethnically, nor politically, and there is only a limited history of institutionalized cooperation among East Asian governments. For the most part East Asian nations have placed more importance on their relations with outside powers than with one another. In the post-colonial era, the cold war provided an international frame of reference in which Asian governments—with some noteworthy exceptions—aligned with Washington, an outsider, against communist governments while concentrating on nation-building and economic development. The United States sponsored the Southeast Asia Treaty Organization (SEATO) in 1954 with Thailand and the Philippines as a link in the global containment of communism, but the organization withered away with the end of the Vietnam War and the American withdrawal from Southeast Asia. After the Korean War, China withdrew to focus largely on itself before slowly opening to the rest of East Asia in the late seventies. Japan was aligned with us but also became an excellent international citizen and poured huge amounts of aid into many other East Asian countries.

ASEAN

The first significant change to East Asia's lack of regional institutions was ASEAN, founded in 1967 at the height of the Vietnam War by Thailand, Indonesia, Malaysia, Singapore, and the Philippines. Shortly after, Walt Rostow, then national security adviser to President Johnson, characterized the establishment of ASEAN to a meeting of American senior officials as a "great world event."

It was hardly that. Designed mostly to help reduce regional tensions among its members, it gained cohesion in the seventies as its members huddled together for mutual comfort and support following the American defeat in Vietnam. It gained credibility on the international stage by helping to reverse the decade-long Vietnamese occupation of Cambodia. It has given its members a somewhat bigger voice in global institutions, including the United Nations, but in general has offered more promise than performance. After many years of discussion, a greater effort to develop economic cooperation began in

1992 when ASEAN governments launched negotiations for a regional free trade area (FTA). Progress has been slow. ASEAN has been
mostly a place for dialogue with an aversion to commentary on the
domestic affairs of its members and a limited involvement in concrete cooperation. ASEAN accepted Brunei in 1984, but its decision
to bring in four new members—Vietnam, Laos, Burma, and
Cambodia—later in the 1990s was at best premature. Expansion did
give window dressing to the concept of "One Southeast Asia," but it
also reduced cohesion, did little for the new members, and complicated
ASEAN decisionmaking.

Out of adversity, however, comes opportunity, and the Asian
financial crisis of 1997–1998 provided that adversity. While ASEAN
as an organization was helpless to solve the problem, the crisis dram-
atized to governments the need for closer cooperation in all of East
Asia, and ASEAN was there to provide a tent pole for such efforts.

THE ASIAN FINANCIAL CRISIS

In our conversations around East Asia, we were struck by how much
the financial crisis of the late nineties still stimulates thinking about
regionalism. It was also a watershed event in East Asian thinking
about the United States.

East Asian countries had suffered financial crises prior to 1997
but never had financial instability spread so rapidly. With national
economies more closely connected to one another and to the rest of
the world, a loss of confidence by global investors in one Asian country could and did lead to an abrupt loss of confidence in others.
International creditors pulled their money out at the first sign of
weakness. The collapse of the Thai baht was followed by speculative flight from the Indonesia rupiah, the Korean won, and other currencies. In just a few months currencies crashed, banking systems
collapsed, companies went belly up, and unemployment rose sharply.

Asians reacted with alarm and bitterness. People saw all that
they had achieved through hard work was suddenly at risk. Many
blamed the United States. There were charges by Asian as well as
Western economists that American-inspired pressures in the early
nineties had caused countries to open their financial markets before
they had created adequate systems of prudential supervision. This in
turn encouraged speculative inflows of short-term funds from abroad

that were vulnerable to capital flight. When the crisis erupted, many Asians felt that the United States was not only slow to respond but also was primarily concerned with protecting Western investors, not saving East Asian economies.

As the crisis spread in the fall of 1997, Washington squelched an incipient effort led by Japan to create a regional facility to provide emergency financial assistance to governments whose currencies were under pressure. Washington chose to rely on the International Monetary Fund (IMF), and governments had no choice but to go along. East Asians commonly regard the IMF as an American domi-nated institution. IMF stabilization agreements themselves came under attack, with charges that Washington took advantage of countries' urgent need for financial assistance to extract commitments for trade and financial liberalization that benefited American business inter-ests. In contrast, China emerged from the financial crisis with its regional cooperation credentials enhanced as many East Asians cred-ited Beijing's decision not to devalue its currency as a major contribu-tion to resolving the regional crisis.

In late 1997, as the financial crisis was exploding, the Asia-Pacific Economic Cooperation forum (APEC), established in 1989 to enhance economic cooperation across the Pacific, held its annual summit in Vancouver. Not surprisingly, the summit provided more irony than solutions for the spreading financial devastation. APEC after all was *the* institution the Americans had championed as an alternative to the East Asia–only model of economic cooperation that Malaysian Prime Minister Mahathir Mohamad promoted in the early nineties and that Washington torpedoed. But APEC was focused on trade liberalization not on international finance. Moreover, its trans-Pacific focus was blurred in the eyes of East Asian governments by the inclusion of sev-eral Latin American nations for whom few Asians felt much affinity. In truth, there was not that much APEC could have done in any case. The Vancouver Summit took place—and the financial crisis spread.

Fairly or unfairly, the crisis marked the beginning of a decline in APEC's political fortunes. Annual summits have continued as have countless meetings of ministers and senior officials, but APEC has lost much of the institutional momentum it had seemingly achieved earlier in the nineties. Most East Asian governments now regard APEC largely as a high-level watering hole, a useful annual opportu-nity for heads of governments to meet but not as a substitute for East

Asia's own regional institutions. U.S. government officials continue to champion it—mostly rhetorically—as "East Asia's most important regional organization."

The financial crisis was politically costly to the United States. Whatever the merits of American emphasis on the need for domestic reform in the region's economic infrastructure—and they were considerable—the Clinton administration failed to see the crisis in the context of its broad strategic interests in East Asia. The crisis may have marked the beginning of a decline in American "soft power" in the region. When we failed to ride quickly to their rescue, we seemed to many in the region to care less about their well-being than we had during the cold war years. The accuracy of this assessment is questionable. But perceptions shape reality, and many in East Asia concluded that protection of their interests required not only better national economic policies but also greater self-reliance and more regional cooperation within East Asia itself.

A New Emerging Regionalism?

In the immediate wake of the financial crisis, ASEAN, prodded mostly by Japan and South Korea, expanded its relations with the three powers of Northeast Asia—China, Japan, and South Korea. In December 1997, the ASEAN members joined Japan, China, and South Korea in the first informal summit of ASEAN Plus Three (APT). In 1999, APT, responding to an initiative of South Korean President Kim Dae Jung, issued a Joint Statement on East Asian Cooperation, a more important event in retrospect than it appeared at the time. For the United States, however, the crisis reinforced what we thought we already knew—that we were dealing with an East Asia made up mostly of new market-oriented economies, and that the challenge was how to continue to integrate them into the global economic system of which we had been the principal steward for decades. We did not challenge or oppose East Asia's post-crisis efforts to create better regional infrastructure, but neither did we show much confidence that regionalism would amount to much.

Now, almost a decade on, APT stands as a working East Asian institution capable of providing concrete help to economies in trouble. APT has developed a comprehensive work program, covering not only finance and economics, but also energy, technology, the environment, and a myriad of other issues that confront govern-ments today. One of the early APT initiatives, launched in 2000 when memories of the crisis were still sharp, was the so-called Chiang Mai Initiative (CMI), which created a network of central bank swap commitments among participating countries. The swap can be activated quickly as a first line of defense against a new finan-cial crisis, and a total of nearly $40 billion is now pledged under the CMI. (The irony is that over the past few years most East Asian countries afflicted by the 1997 crisis have accumulated such large foreign exchange reserves that the likelihood of having to activate the CMI seems low.)

In late 2004, the APT agreed to convene an East Asian Summit (EAS) in Kuala Lumpur in December 2005. And then the debate began. Who would be in? Who would be out? And what would be the agenda? Conceived originally by such nations as South Korea and Malaysia to be the first step toward building an EAC, it was "hijacked" as one prominent Korean put it. Nations like Indonesia wanted a broad attendance, including the United States, to limit China's possible domination of the forum. After a good deal of back-room negotiation, the APT governments expanded the invitation list for the EAS to include India, Australia, and New Zealand, but not the United States. As a rationale for deciding who would be invited, and to make the U.S. absence less pointed, they agreed that the principal condition for participation would be accession to ASEAN's Treaty of Amity and Cooperation (TAC), the pillar of ASEAN's commit-ment to peaceful resolution of disputes. The United States has stated repeatedly and firmly that it would not sign TAC, arguing that the agreement is contradictory to the American security mission in the region. In fact many, perhaps the majority, of East Asia governments did not believe the United States should be invited to the EAS, which they envisioned as a first step toward the creation of a community of and for East Asia. Whether Australia, New Zealand, and above all, India will fit into this amorphous concept of a community remains to be seen. The criteria for membership in an East Asian Community (whether with a large or small "*c*") are far from settled.

The most important fact about the EAS is that it happened. There was no real agenda and only the most general sort of prepara-tion among the governments. In a compromise, APT countries agreed that the EAS would focus mostly on broad security and political

matters, not economic issues. Another three-hour meeting will presumably take place in 2006. That, as many of our interlocutors in the
region note, is the "Asian way." As for an East Asian Community, if
that indeed is what it is called, it is generally expected to take shape
over a period of years and some countries assert that an annual EAS
can play a useful role toward that end. Most important, the APT
will present in 2007 a second joint statement on further East Asian
cooperation that might, some hope, promote a blueprint for an EAC.
Visions, however, vary widely. Japan believes an EAC should consider long-term issues and build around core values like democracy,
rule of law, and human rights. China wants to focus on economic
cooperation. These differences obviously make it difficult at present for governments to offer a grand design for their regional institutions.

More likely, governments will simply try to build on existing elements of cooperation like APT. ASEAN sees itself as the driver for the
effort because neither Japan nor China can take the lead at this point.
The "Three" of the APT will go along, each giving priority to its own
relations with ASEAN countries. It is hard to believe any of the "Three"
will consider the wider community building enterprise to be a major
vehicle for dealing with one another for some time. Whether all this
activity eventually produces an East Asian entity similar in membership
to the APT or a broader more inclusive structure as reflected in the
attendance at the first EAS will depend on many now unforeseeable factors. The realization of either vision will certainly require some level of
reconciliation between Japan and China. We have seen only the first
scene of the first act of what is certain to be a long play.

The substance of East Asian community building will have to
focus on trade and investment, the twin pillars of the region's growing economic integration. Here again, it is hard to predict how
region-wide cooperation might actually evolve. The concept of an
East Asian FTA has been discussed in ASEAN and in the APT.
Thus far the idea has not gained much political traction. There is
presently a proliferation of bilateral trade and investment agreements within the region and between individual East Asian countries and countries outside the region. The United States, for
example, is pursuing an FTA strategy as a hedge against continued
stagnation in the global trade liberalization negotiations known
as the Doha Round on tariff reductions under the World Trade

Organization. As of early 2006, the United States had an FTA with Singapore, one under negotiation with Thailand, and two scheduled for negotiations with South Korea and Malaysia. Regionally, there is a veritable "noodle bowl" of bilateral agreements, with fifteen already in place and nearly three dozen more under negotiations or proposed. What is not clear, however, is whether all these agreements, given their lack of commonality and quite different rules of origin, really facilitate trade. A regional FTA would make a good deal more practical sense and would be an essential underpinning of an EAC. So far, however, this is very much an idea whose time has not yet come, in part because of the tensions among the three big countries in Northeast Asia.

Beyond trade and investment, the focus on further regional economic integration reflects a conviction in many countries of the region that East Asia is entitled to its own regional grouping similar to what the United States already has with its near neighbors in the North American Free Trade Agreement (NAFTA) and recently the Central American Free Trade Agreement (CAFTA) and what the Europeans have in the European Union (EU). We frequently heard that it is time for "Asia to be Asia." In late 2004, former Japanese Prime Minister Yasuhiro Nakasone spoke glowingly to us of regionalism for East Asia despite Japan's troubles with China. We wonder if he still feels that way. This desire to be "Asian" to some extent has similar roots to the discussion a decade ago of so-called Asian values, a discussion that was interrupted by the Asian financial crisis.

The Political Dimensions of Regionalism's Stirrings

China's economic success is changing the regional order. As East Asia becomes more tied into the Chinese economy, Chinese political clout can be expected to rise inside and outside of regional institutions. But there are limits to China's increasing sway. China has prickly neighbors and interdependence is a two-way street. China's position also can be threatened by instability in the neighborhood or by its own hubris. China's rise also unsettles its Asian neighbors as they struggle to find new niches of comparative advantage and worry about how to compete with China in attracting foreign investment. But the process of "creative destruction" marches on, and so far China's neighbors, including Japan, have come to see China more as economic opportunity than as threat. Any substantial disruption of China's economic progress would now spell disaster for the entire region, not just China. All parties should have an interest in creating arrangements that will better tie East Asia together in a web of reciprocal commitments and obligations. That does not mean it will happen.

Not surprisingly, China has changed its approach to the region, particularly in dealing with its Southeast Asian neighbors. In contrast to its behavior in the eighties, it now preaches the virtues of multilateral regional involvement, an inexpensive way to reassure its neighbors that they do not have to fear a powerful China bringing its weight to bear on them one at a time. Conversely, other East Asian nations see regional institutions as a means of "socializing" China, drawing Beijing into a set of obligations and benefits in the same way that China's membership in the WTO, IMF, and other global organizations gives China a stake in observing global norms and developing stronger habits of international cooperation. Certainly, the smaller countries are hoping that multilateral engagement with China will reinforce cautionary impulses in Beijing. Memories in East Asia are long, and virtually all of China's neighbors have some notion of what dealing with a powerful China might be like.

For Japan the calculus is more complicated. Japan has acquired a great economic stake in China; rising exports to China are helping restart Japanese economic growth. As a major investor throughout East Asia, no country has a greater interest in building institutions to help manage better the region's economic interdependence. But Japan has also been the big kid on the block in Asia for much of the second half of the twentieth century; many Japanese are not comfortable with China's economic gains and do not like the prospect of living in China's shadow.

The Japanese are keenly aware that many East Asian countries view them negatively. They are especially aware of Chinese hostility, and they have recent examples of how quickly Chinese governments can whip up anti-Japanese sentiments to pressure Tokyo. For Japan, an East Asian Community can hopefully help calm anti-Japanese feeling in the region and be a buffer against head-to-head competition with China. One Japanese academic told us forthrightly that Japan's "goal is to absorb China into East Asia because China is so big." For some, this is the Jonathan Swift strategy, akin to the Lilliputians tying down Gulliver. Nevertheless, if Japan's economy resurges, it will be less on the defensive. Whether that will affect its enthusiasm for a wider regional institution remains to be seen.

Others with whom we spoke, especially in South Korea, strongly supported regional cooperation. They also saw such cooperation and eventually an East Asian Community as a means of restraining China, although they were not entirely sanguine about the strategy's success. They recall that Gulliver broke free from the shackles of the Lilliputians. They question whether any institutional commitments will check what their collective memories tell them may well be an inexorable Chinese desire to act on its new capability to exercise some degree of "hegemony" over the region. Koreans were incensed about Chinese maps showing the ancient Korean Kingdom of Koguryo as a creature of imperial China. One very senior Southeast Asian leader speculated that in a generation from now, most of Southeast Asia, with the possible exception of Indonesia, would be "under Chinese sway" (without defining what that would really mean). We doubt that East Asian countries will roll over in response to Chinese bullying. Much has changed since the Ming dynasty.

As much as domestic politics, potential leverage, and greater international influence provide an impetus for regional cooperation, they can also be a drag on it. The explosion of anti-Japanese nationalism in the spring of 2005 was sparked initially by Japan's aspiration for a permanent seat on the UN Security Council. The fuel for the fire came from long-standing territorial disputes, the contentious issue of what Japan should teach its children about the thirties and World War II, and the Japanese prime minister's insistence on visiting the Yasukuni Shrine annually. None of these issues have been resolved. Whether they believe it or not, Chinese and Korean politicians and scholars profess to see in Japan's current behavior signs of a return to the prewar Japanese nationalism of the thirties. At the same time the Japanese public's gorge has been rising, and politicians have been delivering public warnings that Tokyo will not buckle to Beijing's manipulation of the history issue. Unfortunately, all this seems to be good domestic politics in each of the three countries and casts a shadow over progress toward East Asian community building.

THE SECURITY DIMENSION

Regional economic integration is not yet changing the nature of security cooperation in East Asia. There is little talk of region-wide East Asian security. Cooperation to date has been generally ad hoc and focused mostly on counterterrorism, piracy in Southeast Asian waters, and U.S. efforts to round up some East Asian nations inter alia in its global Proliferation Security Initiative (PSI) aimed at preventing the smuggling of nuclear weapons materials by North Korea and other miscreants of the NPT.

Since the end of World War II, the U.S. approach to security in East Asia has been to rely on its bilateral alliances. We have never pursued a formal multilateral defense system similar to NATO. Our alliance with Japan remains at the heart of our security strategy for East Asia, just as our commitment to defend South Korea against the North has been crucial to our political credibility and security posture in the region. Since the end of the cold war, our bilateral security ties in Southeast Asia have withered, although we continue to have various training arrangements and access rights in the Philippines, Singapore, and Thailand.

With U.S. encouragement ASEAN spread its wings and created the ASEAN Regional Forum (ARF) in 1994. This relatively young organization brings all of ASEAN's "dialogue partners," including the United States and the countries of Northeast Asia, to an annual meeting of foreign ministers to discuss regional security matters. The United States hoped the institution would help fill some of the security void left by the cold war's end through continuing consultations and would provide a mechanism to reduce chances of conflict in East Asia. The ARF has never gained much traction; it has put pressure on foreign ministers to attend the annual meeting, if only not to be offensive to the others. It provides an opportunity for dialogue, but no one considers ARF an instrument for resolving security issues. Indeed, countries have been largely unwilling to allow substantive discussion of their real security concerns in the area. Internal matters remain off the table.

There has been one significant recent innovation in the regional security arena in Northeast Asia. The Bush administration's distaste for dealing directly with the Kim Jong Il regime coupled with its focus on Iraq led Washington to seek a multilateral approach—a Six-Party process—to negotiate an end to North Korea's nuclear weapons programs. The United States persuaded China to take the lead in organizing the effort, conceding to Beijing a major role in regional security matters for the first time. Whether this new multilateral approach produces results on the Korea issue remains to be seen. (These talks are discussed in greater detail in the next chapter.)

Some form of multilateral handling of North Korea will be needed whatever the outcome of negotiations. If agreement is actually reached, a multilateral structure involving South Korea, Japan, China, Russia, and the United States will be required to provide economic benefits to Pyongyang and help monitor North Korean compliance. If negotiations fail, Washington is likely to press—not necessarily successfully—for a multilateral structure to limit the risk of North Korean exports of nuclear materials, if not more. The creation of the Six-Party talks has also given rise to considerable discussion about a permanent forum for dialogue on security matters among the countries of Northeast Asia and the United States.

Such a permanent forum involving the region's major players might help reduce the friction that our bilateral alliances and relationships germinate. For instance, our efforts to give Japan an expanded role in regional security stimulate Chinese resentment over what they see as encouraging Japanese militarism. That reaction is shared by many in South Korea who fear that they could become the filling in a sandwich with China on one side and the Japanese-U.S. alliance on the other. They do not want to be forced to choose between their long-standing alliance with the United States and their newly important and sensitive relations with China. An ongoing security dialogue in Northeast Asia might at least bring more clarity on such touchy issues as military spending and planning.

WHAT DOES IT ADD UP TO?

Many outsiders find it hard to avoid being skeptical about where the talk of East Asian community building is actually leading. The countries are so different, the languages so many, and the cultural differences vast. Confucianism—the glue of many countries of the region—is being undermined by globalization, and the cooperative experience of the countries of the region is so limited. Nevertheless increased regional cooperation is a natural development, and it is clearly not going away. Most governments apparently think that wider regional cooperation will ultimately have important political and economic benefits; they also believe that they need and deserve their own East Asian cooperative institutions. Yet two broad regional trends are running in different directions. One is toward political and economic integration that is essentially limited to countries in the area and does not include the United States. The other is a continuing concern with regional stability and security where the American role, while different from that it played during the cold war, remains central.

Nevertheless, as we have noted, a goodly number of East Asian nations—not all—believe the United States need not, indeed should not, participate in the evolving construction of an EAC. China is one of them. Yet most are also quick to say that their drive for regional cohesion does not mean they seek to define themselves as being against the United States. The great majority of countries welcome continued U.S. security cooperation and see no contradiction between that and an EAC without the United States—the example of NATO and the EU is often cited.

The inclination to exclude the United States from new East Asian political groupings probably derives in some measure from public dissatisfaction with American policies, especially since September 11 and the invasion of Iraq. This sentiment joins the sentiment that the United States is less committed to the future of East Asia and inclined to define its interests in the region more narrowly than in earlier times. The United States also is seen by many Asians as focusing on the issues dividing Asia, not those bringing it together. All this was brought home to us by a former high-ranking Japanese foreign ministry official who told us flatly that "the U.S. presence in Asia is declining, and self-reliance is the trend in Asia." However pointed that statement, it does not seem to reflect current Japanese policy. Of course, all these attitudes may in the end prove temporary. U.S. insistence on participation in any new regional institution could change things.

Many in the United States are not all that convinced that East Asian regionalism is something that should be taken seriously. They also know that the phenomenon cannot be ignored. We are a Pacific power and have long considered ourselves an integral part of what we like to call the Asian-Pacific region. Over the years, we have preferred to deal with East Asia on a country-by-country basis. That is also how we tend to think about East Asia—one country at a time. In the past, we objected to the creation of pan-Asian institutions of which we would not be a member. Violent American opposition killed Malaysian Prime Minister Mahathir's proposal for a region-wide East Asian economic grouping in the early nineties. The United States argued at that time that as long as it was carrying a heavy security burden in the region, it could not be kept waiting in the corridor when economic matters of great interest to it were being discussed. That argument could still be made.

Most fundamentally, however, East Asia's current movements toward greater regional cooperation occur within a radically different regional context than the early nineties—China's much increased economic and political weight; Japan's relative decline; and the perception, if not the reality, of a United States less politically invested in the region. Meanwhile, Washington is also struggling to find the right balance in its approach to China. Our stance toward deeper and wider East Asian regional cooperation will have to be a part of that balance.

3

THE HOLDOVERS

Given the massive changes in East Asia, it is remarkable that after nearly sixty years the same two issues drive the American security posture in East Asia—Taiwan and North Korea. Once critical areas of competition in the conflict with Mao's China, today they are vestigial appendages of the cold war—real and dangerous nevertheless. The passage of time and the rise of a different China have not brought a resolution any nearer.

The best the United States has been able to do since the Korean War has been to contain these two potential hot spots without hostilities, albeit with plenty of saber rattling on all sides. We have found no silver bullet, but we have produced numerous diplomatic formulas that have helped manage periodic bouts of tension. Coping with these issues is a drain on our resources, our diplomatic capital, and the time and energy of high-level officials. Both issues have roiled our domestic politics and become embedded in partisan political debate, severely limiting any administration's freedom of action on either issue. Along the way, we helped build two prosperous democratic societies in Taiwan and South Korea—no mean achievement.

Taiwan and North Korea are major analytical obstacles to anyone trying to think about the longer-term future of the United States in East Asia. For example, America's interest in preserving the peace in the Taiwan Strait sparks growing concerns about China's military buildup. The uncertainty about how these issues will turn out compounds the difficulty of thinking realistically about future developments in East Asian security and the nature of U.S. involvement in the area. It is nice to speculate about what an East Asia free from these two potential crisis spots might look like, but at this point, one can only guess. It would also be imprudent to take their resolution for granted.

There has been little change in the essence of either problem. Long shorn of its pretensions to regain the mainland, a de facto independent Taiwan wants no part of China, while Beijing remains determined to assert sovereignty and some form of control over the island. North Korea continues to use the perceived threat from American and South Korean forces to justify its militarized, totalitarian regime. Yet each problem has changed in important ways. Taiwan has turned into a thriving democracy, wanting to make its own way in the world, while a much more powerful China can no longer be simply shrugged off as we have for much of the past half-century. North Korea, a charter member of the "axis of evil," has gone backward and its population has been decimated, but it now apparently produces nuclear weapons, which has radically changed American views of the threat it poses. In the meantime South Korea, more confident that it can handle North Korea, insists on pursuing its own political strategy toward the North instead of aligning squarely with the United States. Notwithstanding all the good things occurring in East Asia, the possibility of war still looms.

A Troubled Taiwan

Richard Nixon's 1972 trip to China, as has been often noted, changed the world. The central issue of this visit was Taiwan, and it culminated in the famous Shanghai Communiqué. The United States and China found a formula for leaving the issue of Taiwan's relationship to the mainland effectively to the future under a rubric that was labeled "One China but not now." The United States acknowledged Beijing's claim to "One China," of which Taiwan is a part and agreed not to "challenge that position." This gesture permitted our relationship with China to move forward from hostility to cautious engagement and allowed both countries to focus on the common Soviet threat. It offered the possibility that with the passage of time Chinese pragmatism on both sides of the Taiwan Strait would work its magic and that mainland China and Taiwan would find ways to resolve their differences peacefully. In the ensuing decades, pragmatism and proximity have helped greatly advance the economic integration of Taiwan and China, but domestic politics in both countries have made the political differences between them more complicated and resistant to solution.

While the United States has helped prevent hostilities, it has not actively tried to bring about a settlement. We have been restrained both by our domestic political differences over how hard to press Taiwan and a lack of interest from either side in a more direct American role. U.S. policy has focused on preventing Taiwan from indulging its dangerous tendencies to challenge Beijing openly and go off on its own, while giving China reason to worry about war with the United States if it became truculent and aggressive. At the same time, the United States continues to sell sizable amounts of arms to Taiwan, to reinforce both military deterrence and Taiwan's bargaining position. But Taiwan basically clings to the United States for its defense. Periodically, when tensions seem combustible, the United States has felt the need to apply more fire retardants. The United States had a second "communiqué" with China in 1979, when it broke relations with the national government of Taiwan and recognized the People's Republic of China. A third communiqué in 1982 defused a conflict over our arms sales to Taiwan, and the notion of a fourth is periodically suggested as a way to calm the most recent flare-up.

The Taiwan Relations Act in 1979, in which the United States pledged "to maintain the capacity to resist any resort to force or other forms of coercion that would jeopardize the security or the social or economic system of the people of Taiwan," still serves to prevent the United States from going "wobbly" over Taiwan. U.S. officials hold frequent meetings with both sides and issue firm statements when needed to calm tensions. Some wonder whether this policy framework is still sufficient to keep the issue from unraveling, but American domestic politics precludes serious discussion of alternatives.

IMPERATIVES IN THE TAIWAN STRAIT

Taiwan, of course, has become a prosperous, militarily powerful, and, most important in the context of American domestic politics, a democratic state. Its political parties have their own agendas and constituencies: on Taiwan nationalism, independence, and the status

quo. The central domestic political issue is Taiwan's future relationship to China. Two democratically elected presidents in succession—
Lee Teng-hui and Chen Shui-bian—have tried over the past decade to
break from the One China formula and ultimately to find a way to
establish Taiwan as a de jure recognized independent state. They have
encouraged the development of a "new identity" for Taiwan, one not
linked back to the mainland. So far, however, Taiwan has not gone as
far as either of the two presidents would have wanted had they been
free to do so. They have been held back by domestic and party politics, fear of China's reaction, and American opposition. China has
consigned both presidents to the outer orbit of hell and is now dealing directly with the leaders of the Kuomintang (KMT), Taiwan's
principal opposition party. Since former President Lee's public char-
acterization of cross-strait relations as "state-to-state" in 1999, not to
mention his successor's description in 2002 of their being "one state
on each side" of the strait, Beijing has rejected formal contacts with
the Taiwan government.

Taiwan's voters have shown themselves cautious and not willing to provoke China. But as Taiwan holds more elections, Beijing
reacts more sharply to indications that Taiwan's governing party, the
Democratic Peoples Party (DPP), is trying to boost its electoral
prospects by playing on the independence theme. Beijing also uses
its growing weight and influence to prevent or punish any deviation
in the neighborhood from the One China concept and excoriates
"unofficial" contacts by Asian leaders with Taipei. Beijing continues
to block Taiwan from access to international organizations, even the
World Health Organization. All this incenses the Taiwanese, who
believe their considerable economic and political achievements and
large amounts of foreign aid should bring such access. Indeed, they
should but they do not.

The United States cannot take for granted that some provoca-
tions by Taiwan will not stimulate China to take some form of military action. China obviously does not want a fight with the United
States or to attack its compatriots or create an economic crisis in
Taiwan or China. Beijing periodically feels the need to ratchet up
military pressures to deter politically provocative conduct by Taipei.
Most noticeably, China has placed large and growing numbers of
surface-to-surface missiles in mainland areas adjoining Taiwan. It is
significantly expanding its naval and air capabilities in areas near

Taiwan. The U.S. military increasingly warns that China is intent on acquiring a serious capability to sink American ships in the Taiwan Strait. American concerns over China's rising military capability led to a fierce row with the EU over its intention to end its embargo on sales of sophisticated military equipment to China.

China's leaders would much prefer that the United States get Taiwan to "behave" so they do not have to use more muscular measures. They also want the United States to limit arms sales to Taiwan, both to curb its audacity and weaken its negotiating posture. Taiwan, most of the time but not always, wants more arms as well as continuing reassurance that the United States will in extremis come to the island's defense. Interestingly, however, over the past few years Taiwan has grown reluctant to buy all the arms the United States has offered and insisted on selling. Its resistance is motivated by budgetary considerations and in part by intense domestic political infighting but may also reflect a growing recognition that in the final analysis more than additional military equipment is required to assure the island's security. Taiwanese frugality incenses the Pentagon, which believes Taiwan should not have "a free ride" for its defense and also wants to help maintain the profitability of our defense firms. There is also a strong defense view that Taiwan must be able to defend itself in the face of an attack until the United States can effectively come to its aid. As one looks at the extent of the arms buildup on both sides since 1995, the framework of mutual restraint that has contained the problem for decades seems to have eroded. The buildup on both sides increases the risks and consequences of a misstep.

To avoid giving either side certainty about what it would do if hostilities broke out, the United States tries to maintain ambiguity about its military response. Our public language has been honed by two generations of diplomats, and all the parties are attuned to the slightest nuance. There may well be doubts in both Taiwan and China about the strength of the American commitment to Taiwan, perhaps more so now because of our protracted difficult involvement in Iraq and the way we have responded to North Korea. The Taiwan government obviously will never acknowledge publicly any doubt about a U.S. commitment to Taiwan's defense, though some leaders may well feel the country made a mistake in the late seventies and eighties in buckling to Washington's pressure to stop their secret nuclear weapons program. But the fact remains that U.S. military deployments in the region serve both to reassure Taipei and caution Beijing.

Near crises replete with threats and occasional shifts in military deployments occur periodically. When the authors visited Beijing in mid-2004, the government was in one of its frenzies about Taiwan's "traitorous" President Chen Shui-bian. The foreign minister refused to talk to us about anything except the "crisis," which Taiwan's president was creating. From the minister and every other senior Chinese official we spoke with, we heard the constant refrain that Beijing's immediate goal was not reunification but rather to "curb the independence trend" on the island. It was tough talk, but China was hardly in a warlike mood, and Beijing was focused on sprucing up the city for the 2008 Olympics, which it badly wants to be successful. We were witnessing a little bit of Chinese kabuki.

When we visited Taipei shortly afterward, senior political leaders assured us they do not want to provoke China and would be cautious. They took China's alarms in stride, often referring to its threats with a familiar Chinese proverb: "Lots of thunder, no rain." By October the threats had vanished, and since President Chen's party lost in the December 2004 parliamentary elections, there have been only occasional outbursts of thunder. The Taiwanese electorate may be willing to go part way down the road toward independence, but they clearly do not want to arouse the dragon. This is, however, a never-ending saga. President Chen, in early 2006, reeling from political reversals, was igniting another political storm advocating measures that may rejuvenate his party base but impact negatively on Taiwan's relations with both China and the United States.

DOMESTIC POLITICS

No figure comparable to Mao Zedong and Deng Xiaoping dominates the China scene today. Chiang Kai-shek and Chiang Ching-kuo are also gone from Taiwan. Top officials in both places now have to worry more about domestic politics in order to survive. At some point, despite the common desire to avoid conflict, the amalgam of domestic politics and nationalism in one or both places could become dominant, forcing governments to take steps and countermeasures they really want to avoid.

Taiwan's governing DPP came from behind in the 2004 election to win another presidential term primarily by playing the card of Taiwan nationalism, that is, separation from the mainland. The concept of a distinct Taiwanese identity is now entwined in the island's domestic politics. Even the more cautious, mainlander dominated opposition KMT has had to make some genuflection to this new Taiwan consciousness. As a leading Taiwanese political analyst noted, "Our leaders use the Taiwan independence issue to rally people around them—we call it political Viagra." There is always a risk that some leader may sacrifice Taiwan's national interest by an overconsumption of its cure for electoral dysfunction. Emotional outbursts are always with us.

Clearly, the need for American support is also part of Taiwan's politics and serves as a continuing restraint on rash behavior. But at times, Washington seems to have had trouble getting its cautionary warnings heard by Taiwan's leaders. In 2003, President Bush, in a move that shocked conservative Republicans, publicly rebuked Taiwan's president while in the company of China's premier who was visiting Washington. More cautious presidential speeches and Taiwan's restrained response to China's 2004 Anti-Secession law indicate that U.S. influence in Taipei still counts for plenty. However, the more the United States has to distance itself from Taiwan's leaders, the more Taiwan's strategic position is weakened. Thus domestic politics can ultimately be very costly for Taiwan.

In Beijing the ultimate recovery of Taiwan is regarded as a profound national responsibility for the Communist Party. This is a national conviction, something that few Americans, particularly on the right, can accept. The "sacred duty" to reunite China is a touchstone of Chinese nationalism. Mao said China could wait one hundred years, but as Taiwanese rhetoric has taken a more separatist tone in recent years, China's time horizons have shortened, although its recent Anti-Secession law set aside any sense of time urgency. No Chinese political leader would ever question why Beijing must insist on ultimate unification or rule out a military response should China's territorial unity seem in jeopardy. Few if any will argue for a softer Chinese line toward Taiwan independence, and if a leadership crisis occurs in Beijing, there is always the risk that rival factions would be tempted to compete on the basis of who is toughest on Taiwan. In China, as in the United States, the safest political course is always to go toward the right.

China has been a divisive political issue in the United States since the forties and the dispute over "who lost China." The venom in our China debate has diminished, though certainly not disappeared, since Nixon's visit to Beijing in 1972. Many will recall the hype when the first visiting top Chinese leader, Deng Xiaoping, in 1979 wore a huge grin under an oversized ten-gallon hat. But that was when China was not considered much of a threat to the United States and an ally against the Soviet Union.

The Taiwan issue has excited more Republicans than Democrats, who now concentrate their political rhetoric mostly on the alleged economic threat from China. Legislators of both parties, however, are intent on ensuring that Taiwan is not forced to accept unification. A strongly conservative element in the Republican Party sees China as the only serious long-term threat to American global primacy and supports Taiwan independence as a way to limit China's rise. With so many other difficult problems on its platter, as well as a burgeoning trade relationship with China, and China's importance as a buyer of American debt, the Bush administration has drifted away from its political base on the Taiwan issue. It has sought to deepen relations with China and to avoid difficulties over Taiwan. It has strongly adhered to the One China line. Meanwhile, Taiwan's latitude for playing domestic politics in the United States, once very large, is probably narrowing despite its enormous political skills and fervent supporters. China too has been learning to play the lobbying game in Washington, and it now has plenty of goodies in its bag.

THE LIMITS TO CONFLICT

American strength and diplomatic formulas have facilitated an enormous growth in economic ties between China and Taiwan. There are some four million trips from Taiwan to the mainland each year. Almost a million Taiwan citizens now live in China, and Taiwan investment there has reached $100 billion. Trade between the two now totals over $60 billion. Business executives on both sides chafe at the restrictions Taiwan still imposes on investment. The integration of Taiwan into the Chinese economy complicates decisionmaking in both countries, but it is not yet working to diminish political tensions or produce a serious dialogue.

Indeed, there has been no authoritative cross-strait dialogue of any sort that we know of since 1998, other than barbs punctuated from time to time by modest cosmetic gestures such as allowing direct charter flights for certain Chinese holidays. In April 2005, the world witnessed surprising new developments, which caused consternation in Taipei's government. The top leaders of China's Communist Party met in Beijing with the top leaders of Taiwan's KMT, once its bitter rival for power. Whether this turns out to be a Beijing Spring, leading to serious nonpolemical talks between the two sides, remains to be seen. It was certainly an effort by the KMT to undermine President Chen. So far, little has changed on the island, and no serious discussions have followed. The talks between Beijing and the KMT may have made movement toward independence more difficult, but they also have revived the differences between the Taiwan-born Chinese and those who fled from the mainland. A taboo has been shattered and new hopes have arisen that we may be at the cusp of a new era of the Taiwan issue. For its part, Beijing's interest in better appealing to the people of Taiwan has been limited to those political party talks and some small gestures on agricultural trade and other exchanges.

The authors of this book have long felt that economics would ultimately bridge the chasm, that deepening financial stakes for both countries would prevent nationalist feelings from running amok and lead to a practical, even if secret, dialogue. We are still waiting. There is more that can be done to reduce barriers to trade and travel, although such measures by themselves have not yet changed the atmosphere. Neither Beijing nor Taipei want to give anything away; Taipei is afraid that greater economic ties will reduce the island's room for maneuvering and periodically tries to restrain investment in the mainland. While the people of both countries do not want hostilities and leaders on both sides are likely to be cautious, that may not be enough to avert some sort of military action at some point. This could range from taking an offshore island held by Taipei to a full-scale blockade of Taiwan. The economic consequences of such an action would be horrendous. Indeed, just by turning their talk more bellicose about Taiwan, Beijing could have a serious economic impact on the island.

It is questionable whether maintaining a stable uncertainty helps or hinders a solution in the long term. There is little political interest in the United States—indeed concerted opposition—for changing current policy except for a strong conservative element that wants Taiwan independence. U.S. officials shy away from serious consideration of a new policy, in part because they believe there is little danger of war, and there would be political costs to changing well-established rhetoric. Most lawmakers are disinclined to listen to the worries of China specialists, particularly when the United States wants to sell more and better weapons to Taiwan. There are in fact few China specialists presently arguing for a change in policy or a more active American role.

Nor is there much discussion in the United States about what Taiwan would gain from declaring independence or why the United States should defend Taiwan if it flagrantly disregards American interests and warnings. Maybe Taiwan's leaders hope, if not believe, that our domestic politics would drive the Americans to their defense, but that at some point could be a risky bet. Such concerns do not generate much public attention in Taiwan. Taiwan will likely gain little from independence. Beyond the virtual certainty of triggering some sort of Chinese military action, few countries would recognize Taiwan, and it could well find itself even more isolated economically with huge economic costs. China would also bear serious economic costs if military conflict broke out. But that prospect is not likely to dissuade the Chinese leadership from serious action if worse came to worse. We have some uncertainty where the red lines are in Beijing. There is always some risk that one could be crossed without our even realizing it was there.

Even if China did not immediately go to war, the United States would find itself with huge political and security problems, particularly if Taiwan provoked a major crisis. Many on the right would insist we recognize and defend Taiwan independence, asserting that democracy in Taiwan must have its due and that China must finally recognize reality. This school of thought also apparently believes China has too much to lose to go to war over Taiwan and argues that rather than pushing restraint on Taiwan the United States should press China to accept reality. Others would argue that it is folly to jeopardize our national interest and risk the possibility of war to please Taiwan politicians, who enjoy an autonomy that amounts to de facto independence.

The world is not static and whose side time is on can be argued. Taiwan will some day—perhaps soon—have to decide whether it will begin to deal seriously with Beijing or continue to rely on the hope of

Beijing ultimately being brought low by internal weakness or transformed into something resembling a democracy. If it makes the wrong choice, it could ultimately be left with a weaker hand, which the United States could be less willing to buttress. Similarly, China has to consider how much of an arms race it wants with the United States in the Taiwan Strait. The U.S.-Taiwan connection is more important to the security of Taiwan than the supply of American arms. But politicians rarely gamble for an uncertain future to replace a tolerable here and now. All the governments involved still hope that something will turn up, but they also expect that the present situation will remain quiet if the United States maintains its current approach.

CAN WE DEAL WITH NORTH KOREA?

Just as Taiwan has changed radically, so too has North Korea—but mostly for the worse. As in the early nineties, we are again absorbed with stopping North Korea's nuclear weapons programs. After waiting expectantly for a North Korean collapse for several years, Washington still mostly looks at the country as if its leader, Kim Jong Il, were certifiable despite evidence of his short-term cunning, whatever his long-term failures.

North Korea is a totalitarian state, where rule may pass to a third generation of the Kim family. It is the most opaque state in the world. Our intelligence community tries hard, but it knows little about the inner workings of the country and how decisions are made. We can depend on being surprised by what happens in North Korea.

Economically ahead of its southern brethren until the seventies, the North has fallen light years behind. Always a brutal state, it is now a failed state. Its military consumes much of its diminished national product. Well over two million North Koreans have died from famine. Many of its citizens have fled the country and live perilously in northeast China. With Beijing providing only a portion of the aid that used to come from the Soviets, North Korea is heavily dependent for its survival on foreign assistance and earnings from weapons exports, drug trafficking, and counterfeiting.

After many years of economic contraction and frequent famine, North Korean leaders have finally acknowledged—implicitly—that their system does not work. Kim Jong Il periodically takes off for

China, apparently to study the Chinese economic model, but he is yet to embrace it. The government recently introduced limited economic reforms, freeing some prices and wages, tolerating public markets, and permitting more individual initiative, including the ownership of land. South Korea has been allowed to set up a sizable industrial zone on the northern edge of the Demilitarized Zone, where its companies make use of inexpensive North Korean labor. Today, North Korea is a little more open and, according to visitors, a bit more lively.

None of these recent measures has yet generated much growth. North Korea's agricultural production always seems an annual uncertainty, and its energy problems keep growing. Although South Korean private investment and Chinese advice seem to be having some psychological impact, real reform in North Korea would require more fundamental change in the way it operates and greater opening to the outside world. Kim Jong Il and company fear—probably correctly—that significant changes would lead to a loss of control and endanger their rule. Even under the terribly difficult economic circumstances of the nineties, a loss of control has never occurred, although we will never know how close the country may have been to actually falling apart.

For years our principal security preoccupation on the Korean Peninsula has been to deter or—if deterrence fails—to defeat a conventional North Korean attack on the South. A briefing from the American military command in Seoul can still call up images of fierce North Korean forces revving their tank engines and firing long-range artillery and short-range missiles at Seoul, where tens of millions of Koreans live. But a conventional war has become an unlikely contingency. North Korea is not suicidal. Its leadership knows that while it can inflict substantial damage on the South, the relative strength of its conventional forces has declined substantially, and a conventional attack would almost certainly lead to the destruction of the regime. That does not mean that North Korean missiles and artillery arrayed against Seoul no longer constitute a formidable capability for blackmail. They do. But the shift in the balance of conventional forces does help explain North Korea's emphasis on developing nuclear weapons as a more effective deterrent to an American attack.

A core component of the North Korean mindset is a massive mistrust of the United States, which infects every aspect of its policies and shapes its very existence. North Koreans are to some extent the victims

of their own propaganda, which has for decades justified the depriva-
tion and militarization of North Korean society by warning that if
they let down their guard even slightly, the United States and its pup-
pets in the South will smash them.

The initial rhetoric of the Bush administration significantly reinforced this North Korean worldview. The quick overthrow of Saddam
Hussein probably made North Korea even more fearful of an
American attack, and although its nuclear weapons program began
several decades ago, it likely now views nuclear weapons more than
ever as the only sure way to stay the American hand. On the other
hand, the American morass in Iraq today must lessen North Korea's
concern about the "nefarious" Mr. Bush and the imminence of an
American attack. Pyongyang might express a willingness to negotiate
away its nuclear programs, but many specialists believe it will never
do so.

Meanwhile South Korea, a tumultuous democracy with the
world's eleventh largest economy, after many decades of reinforcing
North Korea's isolation now helps keep Pyongyang going with large
doses of grain, fertilizer, and occasionally, cash. South Korean private investment in the North is growing despite the complexity of
doing business there. After Kim Dae Jung became president in 1998,
the South Korean government began to pursue a strategy toward the
North based on the proposition that reconciliation and even peaceful
reunification were achievable, though probably not the latter for a
long time. Kim's approach, known as the "Sunshine Policy," sought
to "engage" North Korea, using the leverage of the South's economic superiority to make the North more and more dependent on Seoul.
While the South Korean government does not talk much about it
publicly for obvious reasons, the Sunshine Policy also was predicat-
ed on the belief that the dependency created by the South's economic largesse would over time create fissures and tensions within the
ruling elites in the North and soften the regime's hard-line approach
to the world.

The current president, Roh Moo Hyun, has stepped up the
Sunshine Policy with much greater economic assistance. Above all,
President Roh wants to avoid a crisis over North Korea's nuclear pro-
grams lest it scare off investors, undermine the South Korean economy,
and jeopardize his ability to bring greater equality and social justice to
South Korea, a goal he considers central to his legacy.

THE AMERICAN RESPONSE AND ITS PROBLEMS

The Bush administration changed American policy on Korea. The engagement with North Korea of the last year of the Clinton era was out. North Korea became "a rogue state" and, after September 11, a charter member of the "axis of evil," accurate characterizations of the nature of the North Korean state but not conducive to negotiations. When it first assumed office, the Bush administration did not want to talk to North Korea at all. Bowing to South Korea's urging, it seemed eventually prepared to hold its nose and resume bilateral talks of some sort with Pyongyang, even as it decried Clinton's policy as feckless. It said it would never submit to North Korean extortion as it charged the Clinton administration did in the 1994 U.S.–North Korean Agreed Framework, which traded North Korea's commitment to freeze and eventually dismantle its plutonium program for a package of economic benefits, notably two light water reactors and heavy fuel oil. Importantly, the Agreed Framework also provided something of a blueprint for better relations between Washington and Pyongyang and eventually between Pyongyang and Seoul. The Bush administration insisted, however, on a "comprehensive" approach to the North, including not only nuclear weapons but also such issues as conventional force reduction and improving human rights, which was not much of an inducement for the North.

The two sides finally resumed talks in late 2002, but the surfacing of new intelligence pointing to the existence of a secret North Korean program to produce highly enriched uranium (HEU) added to the negative atmosphere that surrounded U.S.–North Korean relations. The United States confronted North Korea on the HEU program in October 2002. Pyongyang first reportedly admitted to an HEU program and then denied it. The facts are murky, but unlike intelligence on Iraq, the U.S. government was united in its view that the North had serious nuclear weapons programs going. The Agreed Framework rapidly came apart. Washington, supported by Tokyo and, after some hesitation, Seoul, suspended compliance with its obligations under that agreement, including construction of two light water reactors in North Korea. Pyongyang in turn threw out the UN inspectors from its frozen plutonium facility, walked away from the Nuclear Non-Proliferation Treaty (NPT), and resumed its production of plutonium.

After September 11, fear grew in Washington that, given its poverty and pursuit of nuclear weapons, North Korea might sell weapons materials or even actual nuclear weapons to terrorists or other "rogue states" for badly needed cash. Credible or not, that fear elevated North Korea to near the top of America's agenda of worries, although administration actions to deal with what seemed an imminent threat of a larger nuclear weapons capability in North Korea fell far short of the response to fears of WMD in Iraq. Indeed, Bush has continued to say he "can be patient" with North Korea, no doubt in great part because North Korea raises far more complexities for a military solution than Iraq seemed to in 2003. His patience seems to continue.

Washington fostered a unique multilateral (Six-Party) negotiating forum, consisting of Japan, China, the two Koreas, Russia, and the United States, to try to end North Korea's nuclear weapons programs. The rationale for the new diplomatic process was that all parties in the region, not just the United States and South Korea, have an abiding interest in getting rid of nuclear weapons on the Korean Peninsula and that North Korea was more likely to give up its weapons and less likely to cheat on any agreement if all its neighbors were involved together with the United States. In a dramatic break with past practice, the United States gave China the helm, and Beijing brought North Korea to the six-sided table in 2003. The multilateral nature of the Six-Party process enabled Washington to reassure domestic conservative critics that we were not dealing bilaterally with the morally contemptible Kim Jong Il regime. Indeed, Washington prevented the first American negotiator from having any serious private conversations with his North Korean counterpart. The other four countries believed bilateral negotiations between the United States and North Korea would ultimately be needed if agreement were to be reached, but they were happy to have any negotiations under way if only to prevent what they feared would be rash American behavior.

Negotiations made little headway. For more than a year—between mid-2004 and mid-2005—it was not even possible to reconvene the talks. But in the second Bush term, policy toward negotiations with the North seemed to change. A new negotiator, former ambassador to South Korea Christopher Hill, was given the freedom actually to talk seriously and privately to his North Korean counterparts. Senior figures stopped sniping publicly at the idea of negotiating with Pyongyang. In September 2005, the Six-Party talks produced a preliminary agreement, a "Joint Statement of Principles" (known hereafter as the September agreement), under which North Korea would end its nuclear weapons programs in exchange for aid and security assurances and recognition of its status as an equal sovereign state.

Washington could probably have realized this agreement on principles earlier had it chosen to do so, although President Bush did add an important dimension with the Six-Party talks. A lot changed since 2003 of course—read Iraq. The Bush administration apparently concluded it had enough on its foreign policy platter without adding a crisis with North Korea, and the Six-Party talks served to reduce the urgency of dealing with the North Korean nuclear issue. Whether the September agreement will lead to a complete agreement remains to be seen. It also remains unclear whether either party really wants a negotiated agreement. North Korea may be just playing for time and the departure of the Bush administration. And many suspect the Bush administration still prefers regime change to a negotiated solution. The September agreement may turn out to be little more than an interesting scrap of paper. As of this writing, the North Koreans have once again stalled the talks supposedly because of American public charges of counterfeiting U.S. dollars and reducing its access to international banks.

Each side has to make a strategic decision if a serious and durable agreement is to be achieved. North Korea has to conclude that it can survive without a nuclear deterrent and that there is an achievable package of aid and reliable security assurances that enhances its prospects for survival. The United States has to conclude that there is a negotiable arrangement, including sufficiently rigorous international inspection, that will give it confidence that North Korea is abiding by its commitment to abandon its nuclear weapons programs.

Why Have We Had so Much Difficulty?

First, our intelligence on North Korean nuclear programs is still limited, and there is not much hope of great improvement. North Korea is a tough intelligence target, perhaps the toughest of all targets. The intelligence community has been wracked with disputes over what North Korea is really doing in the nuclear field. For over a decade, the community has judged that the North "probably" has one or two weapons, but the bottom line is that Pyongyang has not conducted a nuclear test, so we do not know conclusively if North Korea has any nuclear weapons at all, at least ones that work.

We do know that North Korea's plutonium program has had the physical potential to produce fissile material for nuclear weapons, even though no one knows for sure what they have done since they banished the UN inspectors. Estimates vary, but it is generally believed that over the past three years North Korea had the ability to produce enough plutonium for six to twelve nuclear devices on top of the one or two they were believed to have produced previously. We also know little about North Korea's HEU program, the issue that fractured the Agreed Framework in 2002, other than that the North obtained some equipment and materials from Pakistan and other sources.

Without clear intelligence, the United States has little choice but to proceed as though it believes North Korea's assertion that it has nuclear weapons and to be prepared to take whatever preventive action it can, such as through our Proliferation Security Initiative (PSI) aimed at stopping any North Korean nuclear material exports. At the same time, however, without better intelligence, especially given our woeful intelligence performance on Iraq, it has been difficult to speak with authority in the Six-Party talks on the extent of North Korea's nuclear programs.

Second, while all the other five parties, including North Korea, agree that the peninsula should be free of nuclear weapons, each party has a different approach to achieve that end. The U.S. government has defined the North Korean nuclear programs as virtually an existential issue, and professes itself haunted by the specter of leakage of North Korean nuclear materials to groups that would not hesitate to destroy American cities. Given that threat, as some in Washington argue, there is little the United States should ultimately not be prepared to do.

For South Korea and China, and to a lesser extent Russia, the way Pyongyang is separated from its nuclear weapons matters much more. South Korea would be devastatingly affected by war on the Korean Peninsula. Moreover, neither South Korea nor China want to see an early collapse of the Pyongyang regime, fearing the instability and massive disruption that would ensue. They do not want to isolate

North Korea or to take major punitive steps against it if negotiations fail. Not surprisingly, there have been times during the Six-Party talks when skepticism that Washington is prepared to accept a negotiated solution has caused almost as much angst in South Korea as has North Korean intransigence. Above all, South Korea is not prepared under any circumstance to risk war in order to pressure North Korea to give up its nuclear programs. For South Koreans, the North's nuclear weapons, however dangerous, are not an immediate threat. The consequences of an effort to eliminate the North's nuclear programs by force are, on the other hand, very real indeed.

The American commitment to South Korea's defense has been the cement of the U.S.–South Korean alliance, and the United States still expends substantial resources to preserve military deterrence. In recent years, however, many South Koreans have come to see the alliance as still important but less vital to their country's survival. As the economic gap between North and South has widened to a chasm, South Koreans generally have come to see a diminished threat from their northern cousins. Democratization and urbanization have also combined to make South Koreans less tolerant of the still jarring presence of foreign troops, even American ones, on their soil. Strains in the alliance have been greatly exacerbated by the American posture toward North Korea and the way it has handled the Six-Party talks, at least until recently. Many in South Korea, particularly younger generations, have seen the U.S. approach as rigid and threatening to their peace and stability. There are other more conservative voices deeply distrustful of the North and the way the present government is managing relations with the United States and North Korea. Attitudes can change—sometimes quickly—as purely domestic issues affect the fortunes of political parties.

Whatever the public rhetoric of the two governments—that nothing has changed in the alliance—the profound differences over how to deal with North Korea have created a real split, made serious dialogue harder, and profoundly complicated the already difficult task of resolving the North Korean nuclear problem. These differences have also spilled over into public opinion. Some American national security commentators have even declared the alliance effectively dead.

China has long been frustrated with North Korea. While Beijing has publicly expressed skepticism that North Korea has produced nuclear weapons or has a HEU capability, it wants North Korea to change its ways and give up its nuclear weapons programs. The leadership in Beijing has also invested its prestige in the Six-Party process and wants the negotiations to succeed. It has badgered and bribed Pyongyang to participate and be reasonable; Beijing was instrumental in keeping negotiations going over the past three years and in producing the September agreement. But the frequent intimation by senior American officials that China should be willing to put material pressures on North Korea and force a settlement has not been borne out. Indeed, China has been critical of what it sees as American unwillingness to negotiate seriously and has at times pressured Washington to be more flexible.

China has roughly the same approach as South Korea toward Pyongyang: it fears a collapse and wants to make North Korea a more successful, more acceptable state. It provides essential support, particularly the provision of oil and food, even as Chinese elites increasingly treat Pyongyang with disdain. They want North Korea to adopt their market-oriented model for growth. While we would not preclude serious Chinese economic pressures to stop flagrant North Korean behavior—say a nuclear test—we remain skeptical that the Chinese will put all their chips on the table with Pyongyang to secure a nuclear weapons agreement. In any case, the United States cannot rely on it. What has been happening on the ground certainly does not support any notion of Chinese willingness to force Pyongyang into line.

Nor is another former North Korean ally—Russia—chomping at the bit for forced change in North Korean policies. The Russians say all the right things about eliminating the North's nuclear weapons program, but prefer an incremental strategy. They fear North Korea's reaction to strong pressures, and Moscow too seeks a slow transition, not a collapse.

Only Japan has given the United States real support for ratcheting up pressure on the North. Tokyo and Washington are far more worried about North Korea's nuclear and missile capabilities than any of the other powers. Indeed, the Japanese increasingly consider North Korea to be a direct and dangerous threat to their country. This perception, together with an ongoing controversy over the fate of a dozen or so Japanese kidnapped by North Korea many years ago, has hardened Japanese attitudes toward Pyongyang and largely closed Japan's pocketbook. But Tokyo too is cautious in supporting heavy economic or military pressures on Pyongyang. Its enthusiasm for a hard line is tempered by North Korean missiles—possibly capable of carrying nuclear warheads—which are deployed and have Japanese cities in range.

THE DIFFERENT ROADS AHEAD

No American government can ignore the North Korean nuclear issue. The risks to our interests are too great, and in any case, domestic politics would preclude it. There are essentially three ways of dealing with the problem

The first is, of course, the present Six-Party negotiations. Negotiations were the choice in 1994, the first time we dealt with the nuclear problem. After much huffing and puffing and threats of war, a bilateral agreement (the aforementioned Agreed Framework) was reached. From the beginning there were major differences between Washington and Pyongyang's assessments of the balance of benefits in the Agreed Framework. For North Korea, its energy parts—the delivery of fuel and the building of two light water reactors—were important as a test of American good faith. Also very important was the promise that the agreement would lead to a normal bilateral relationship with the United States through the establishment of diplomatic relations, the lifting of economic sanctions, and so forth. North Korea may have hedged against the failure actually to improve relations with the United States as envisioned by starting an HEU program with help from Pakistan, a violation of the Agreed Framework.

For the United States the Agreed Framework was largely a way to get rid of North Korea's known nuclear weapons program. When the Clinton administration confronted stiff Republican opposition in the Congress to the Agreed Framework, it chose to invest little political capital in improving bilateral relations with North Korea. Washington's policy seemingly consisted largely of waiting for the widely expected collapse of the North Korean regime. That course was no longer politically possible after August 1998, when North Korea captured everyone's attention with a long-range missile shot over Japan and out into the Pacific. That led to a major American effort, including a visit to Pyongyang by Secretary of State Madeleine Albright, to try to resolve the continuing problems, but it was stopped by the election schedule.

The Americans and the North Koreans have accused each other of failing to carry out the 1994 agreement. Nevertheless, for eight years the agreement prevented North Korea both from processing its existing spent fuel into plutonium and from producing new spent fuel from other reactors. In retrospect, it is remarkable that North Korea asked for so little in compensation for suspending its nuclear weapons program—essentially the reactors and some heavy fuel oil. Perhaps they thought that after the reactors were delivered they could find some excuse for walking away from the agreement. Or just possibly, what they wanted most was in fact a more normal relationship with the arch enemy, the United States.

In any event, all the North Koreans ended up getting was some half-billion dollars in heavy fuel oil, a lot of reinforced concrete in a huge hole in the ground, and some temporary relief from the fear of American military attack. Democrats have hailed the Agreed Framework as a successful "marriage of force and diplomacy." Republicans have assailed it as craven blackmail. As the authors see it, the agreement was a relatively inexpensive but temporary success, probably impossible to carry to completion because the parties never developed any trust.

After almost three years, we have reached agreement only on the broad elements of a bargain, but the all important details have to be filled in. In the meantime, North Korea proceeds with its weapons programs while it receives sizable aid from South Korea and China, reducing the incentive to reach an agreement. The Bush administration continues to treat the threat of a nuclear North Korea with no great sense of urgency, lacking an alternative strategy and over committed in Iraq. We do not know how long that will continue.

We also do not know whether North Korea is really prepared to give up its nuclear weapons programs—Kim Jong Il may not have made up his mind—or what the United States and its friends would ultimately pay for it. The world still awaits serious detailed proposals by both sides, particularly over the sequencing of an agreement and its verification. Opaque North Korea is not likely to agree to the openness the United States would require. Whether this could turn out to be a deal breaker remains to be seen, but any "ambiguous" outcome could be taken hostage by our domestic politics. Clearly, a Republican administration will find it easier to defend an agreement than a Democratic one, certainly before a Republican-controlled

Congress. Implementation on both sides could be even more diffi-cult than the 1994 agreement.

But no matter how comprehensive and intrusive the inspection regime, there will always be some uncertainty as to whether Pyongyang is cheating. North Korea is a country filled with caves and tunnels, and has lied or deceived incessantly. The level of ambiguity with which the Bush administration—or for that matter any American administra-tion—will be prepared to live remains to be established.

A second option is for the United States to destroy North Korean nuclear facilities—supposedly what the Clinton administration was going to do in 1994 if no agreement was reached. It continues to be advocated in some quarters in the United States, and neither candidate in the 2004 presidential campaign ruled it out. Our officials contin-ue to love to talk about "all options" being on the table. Maybe, but we doubt it.

A military approach has two drawbacks. First, it is unlikely to destroy all North Korean nuclear programs and existing weapons, especially since we apparently do not know where they are. It could, however, delay progress in their weapons efforts. Second, many fear it would lead to a conventional war. Any American military preemp-tive action would have to be taken over the violent opposition of South Korea, which has the most at stake, including its people and its economy. China also would be strongly opposed, though what it would do in the case of such an action is uncertain. Likewise we can-not be sure how North Korea would react. Would Pyongyang start a war that would likely lead to its destruction? Since it does not want to be destroyed, it is not clear that a full-scale conventional war would automatically follow a preemptive strike. Some sort of retaliatory action, however, would seem likely, lest Kim Jong Il lose all credibil-ity with his own military leaders. There is a grave risk that the situa-tion would quickly get out of control.

The third approach would be to change the regime. This was indeed the Bush administration's preferred policy toward the North for some time, and may still be, even if not explicitly avowed. A few months after he took office, Bush effectively told South Korean President Kim Dae Jung that Kim Jong Il is a bad man and that South Korea was wrong to deal with his terrible government. The administration wanted to pursue regime destruction by isolating North Korea and exerting great economic and political pressures on it. Some senior officials even believed—wrongly—that they could enlist China in an effort to change the North Korean government. This approach has at least one major problem. Fearful that it would lead to war or chaos on their borders, neither China nor South Korea is willing to join us. As it turned out, at the same time President Bush has been trying to isolate Pyongyang, our treaty-ally, South Korea, has been shoveling large sums of money to the North—over $1 billion in 2005 and double that amount planned for 2006.

Another way to try to change the regime or at least its nature and behavior is through a long-term process of engagement. This has been the avowed policy of South Korea and, less explicitly, China. Most other states in East Asia would probably support it. South Korea's engagement strategy seeks to reduce the isolation of the North Korean state by increasing its connection to the outside world through economic assistance, technical help, training, and involving it in more international activities. Seoul's explicit goal has been reconciliation, not the transformation of North Korea, although the South Koreans probably believe nonviolence and efforts toward reconciliation advance the possibility of transformation. China wants the North to adopt or at least move in the direction of its market approach and plies Pyongyang with advice and assistance. So far, while there have been modest changes in North Korean economic policy, there is no sign of transformation or even any lessening of the hostility and suspicion with which North Korea treats the outside world.

Many Americans believe South Korea's approach is futile and would, at best, produce results only in the very long term. Giving them aid can be an endless exercise, particularly if there are no penalties. Some believe it is immoral to extend any benefits to such a reprehensible regime. But the basic problem with the approach is that by itself it does little to stop North Korea's nuclear efforts. For the United States at least, such a long-term approach needs to be accompanied by a verifiable nuclear agreement.

So far the Six-Party negotiations may have served to constrain the Americans as much as the North Koreans. That will not change until and unless it becomes clear to all parties that a credible negotiated agreement is not possible. Even then, the threat of tough American action, more economic pressure, or the rattling of B-2s is more likely to send China and South Korea scurrying than to cause North Korea to become "reasonable."

While the September agreement is welcome, as of this writing it has not been followed up. The authors are skeptical that in the end Kim Jong Il will give up his nuclear weapons. There is so much distrust between the two governments that reaching a satisfactorily verifiable agreement is exceedingly difficult, and American domestic politics probably make a less than perfect agreement, whatever that might be, unsustainable. Short of an act of God in North Korea, the nuclear issue is likely to be with us for some time to come. That probably means that we will have to live with a nuclear-armed North Korea. The alternative may well be that at some point there will be a dangerous crisis not only with North Korea, but with our friends, South Korea and China.

4

KEEPING THE PEACE
AMERICAN POWER IN A
CHANGING EAST ASIAN CONTEXT

With the exception of North Korea, the big countries of Northeast Asia, where the military might in East Asia is, are doing well. They are focused mostly on internal change and economic growth. Their strengthening economies are increasingly integrating with one another as well as with the rest of the region and the rest of the world. The Taiwan Strait and North Korea, of course, remain among the most dangerous problems in the world. But North Korea and Taiwan aside, it is difficult to envision realistic circumstances, including territorial disputes and Japan-China tensions, that would cause countries in East Asia to come to serious blows. In Southeast Asia the principal security problems are internal stability, Islamic extremism, and low-level violence, as will be seen in the next chapter.

PERCEPTIONS OF POWER

American global preeminence is not likely to diminish significantly for at least a generation and perhaps even longer. No other country has the combination of economic strength and a political willingness to maintain the high levels of military spending that would be required to challenge it militarily on a global basis. The United States is also a major, if not dominant, power in every region around the globe. In

East Asia, the United States has been *the* regional power since the end of World War II. But change is under way.

While there still is a healthy respect for American military power in East Asia, there is some uncertainty about the relevance of that power in terms of what is actually happening in the area. One small indicator of change is the status of CINCPAC, the Commander in Chief, Pacific Command, responsible for U.S. forces in the Pacific. For much of the past fifty years, CINCPAC was a major personality in the area. He met routinely with heads of state, and doors were open to him. The press was usually at his heels, and he was a symbol of American power. But there has been no war in East Asia for a generation, and today many fewer Asians know what a CINCPAC is, much less who occupies the post. Indeed, the Defense Department recently changed his title to Commander, U.S. Pacific Command, something of a comedown.

Nevertheless, many East Asian governments still prefer a robust American military presence in the area. Most believe that U.S. forces in Northeast Asia are critical to keeping the peace in Korea and the Taiwan Strait. But even some of our stronger allies in East Asia want some restructuring of the American military presence to reduce its political profile in their countries. The marines in Okinawa remain a particularly thorny problem for both the American and Japanese governments; the U.S. military, after years of discussion, will finally be moving out of Seoul. Some countries wonder about the value of American power, and their populations are wary, if not hostile, about how the United States has been using its military might elsewhere in the world. In other words, today governments in East Asia usually find comfort in having the Seventh Fleet just over the horizon, but they are not always eager to see American ships steaming into their ports.

This changing perspective flows in great measure from China's growing economic and military power. Even for those Asian nations who worry about being bullied by China, there is not much of a sense of any active Chinese military threat—except in Taiwan—that needs to be deterred by the American military presence, although many in Japan look very far down the pike. China's neighbors, on the other hand, do realize that their hopes for economic growth and stability are in large measure dependent on good ties with China. If China prospers, they will prosper, and if China is hurt, they will be hurt. There is, in short, a new complexity about what counts in East Asia.

Some important Americans see China differently. For example, Secretary of Defense Donald Rumsfeld, a master of the pithy sound bite, made a strong China statement at the 2005 security conference in Singapore attended by defense chiefs and other luminaries from East Asia and elsewhere. Rumsfeld characterized China's investment in new weapons systems as a threat to Asian countries and went on to ask: "Since no nation threatens China, one must wonder: Why this growing investment?" Rumsfeld lowered his tone in a later visit to China—his first in five years as defense secretary—but raised again his anxiety over what he believes is China's rapid and striking military modernization.

Rumsfeld's question is an important one, but it could be asked of all countries that maintain large and costly defense establishments. Moreover, coming from the defense chief of a country that spends more on defense than the rest of the world combined, one whose vast strategic forces are being redirected to China, and one that, while having legitimate security concerns, has been prone to spending huge amounts of money on questionable threats, Rumsfeld's question—in its boldest terms as in Singapore—borders on the ludicrous. In part, his question reflects a deeply held belief in some quarters of the American foreign policy establishment that the United States has unique burdens and responsibilities, which everyone must of course recognize, and that these require a huge military edge everywhere in the world. Since we are the good guys who ride to the rescue of the weak and oppressed, any amount we spend on defense is justified, and, whatever we do, we should not be seen as a threat to anyone who does not have malign intentions. That is, of course, not always how other countries have seen us. Rather, many see a country that has enormous military power and has demonstrated a willingness to use that power whenever it judges it necessary to its own interests without much reference to the views of the rest of the world. Americans may consider that a harsh or irrelevant judgment, but it is the perception in much of East Asia, if not the world.

Rumsfeld's question also reveals a mindset in the Pentagon about China and its prospective challenge to American preeminence, a mindset that is growing in Washington and elsewhere in the country. While few disagree that our relationship with China is multi-dimensional, China is often viewed as a rising power consumed by an innate urge to regain control over Taiwan, stirring a historical rivalry with Japan, scheming to take disputed islands in the Pacific, oppressing its own minority populations, and wanting "to drive the United States out of Asia," whatever that famous phrase means given the magnitude of China's trade surplus with the United States. There is also a deeper belief, particularly among the conservative cognoscenti, that an increasingly powerful, nondemocratic China will ultimately challenge the existing world order, which has been largely constructed by the United States. (An irreverent observer might ask what role model the United States gives China about the need to follow international norms, including the use of force.) This overall assessment—exaggerated as it may be—threatens to shape our thinking about East Asian security and the policies the United States pursues there.

In the United States, the potential threat from China is more and more seen as the critical security issue of future decades. There is a focus on China's growing military power, especially as it may affect our ability to maintain peace in the Taiwan Strait.

In fact, the United States and China have begun to bump up against each other in many fields and many regions—from Uzbekistan to Saudi Arabia, from Iran to Nigeria. This not surprisingly frightens some Americans. It is just not how we have been accustomed to think about China.

DEVELOPMENTS IN AMERICA'S SECURITY POSTURE IN THE AREA

The United States must have a comprehensive global security strategy that fits together all the various parts, regional and domestic. Decisions on our security posture in East Asia have to be based not only on our broad policies and interests in that region but also on our global needs. For the past four years, the Bush administration has been reassessing our worldwide deployments and basing structure, including those in East Asia. This reassessment is driven in part by heightened concerns over countries where terrorists gather or might gather in the future and where we might one day need to use force. For these and other contingencies, we need military forces that operate from platforms of high technology and are rapidly deployable everywhere. As a practical matter, this is not a doctrine that can be unilateral. In East Asia, as well as in other regions, these operating principles require transit rights, training facilities, port access, and perhaps even basing privileges. This means, of course, that we need friends and allies in the region, though we also will emphasize the greater use of American territories like Guam for our deployments.

The present American military posture in East Asia is responsive to the two major military contingencies—North Korea and the Taiwan Strait—that still persist. It also tries to be consistent with our emerging global policy of "strategic flexibility," the ability to respond quickly and not to have forces tied down to use for only one contingency. Since the end of the cold war, the United States has whittled down its forces in the area, particularly in South Korea. The judgment has been that as the South's military capabilities have strengthened and the North's economic decline has eroded its conventional military strength, the United States could afford to reshape its presence, relying more on technology and airpower and less on ground troops. Overall this case is compelling, unlike President Carter's effort to remove all U.S. ground forces from South Korea thirty years ago. The Korean government has also agreed to spend $11 billion in force improvements to make up for the reduced American military capability.

The Pentagon believes it can no longer afford to have American forces in South Korea limited to the task of deterring North Korea; our forces should be available for contingencies outside South Korea—even though it never identifies any of those contingencies explicitly.

For South Koreans, strategic flexibility raises troubling questions, especially as it becomes a subject of public discussion in Seoul. Some Koreans worry that a reduction of American force levels weakens deterrence. Others ask whether American forces in South Korea are to be used elsewhere in East Asia. Against whom and under what circumstances? What South Koreans fear is that continued U.S. deployments in their country can be part not just of a strategy for dealing with contingencies in Southeast Asia or beyond but rather of an emerging strategic posture toward China. They fear this could at some point put them in a political vise between Washington, their long-time ally, and Beijing, a vital economic partner and the neighborhood's new big guy. In South Korea and probably in China too, the doctrine of strategic flexibility seems to reflect an assumption that the United States will need forces in South Korea for a long time, whatever happens in North Korea. In fact, we may have drifted into this assumption without adequate analysis of the changing strategic context of Northeast Asia.

U.S. officials sometimes justify the need to maintain forces on the Korean Peninsula as being politically important to the greater strategic need to keep our forces in Japan. The argument runs that the Japanese government must be able to show to its people that it is not the only Asian country that welcomes an American military presence. That begs the question of what kind of forward deployments we need overall in Northeast Asia given threats that now exist or may emerge in the future. At times, it seems as though little has changed in our strategic thinking since the end of the cold war: forward deployments are important in themselves and for our overall influence, and new rationales are needed only to mollify East Asian governments and secure the cooperation of publics. Our justification seems to be that we need them because the world is uncertain, which of course it is, but hardly an illumination for policymaking.

CHINA

Probably the most important question in international affairs in the first half of this century will be what happens in China and what China does in the world, although some would put turmoil in the Middle East at the top. China is critical to our efforts to end North Korea's nuclear weapons programs and to maintain peace in the Taiwan Strait. It has become a major American preoccupation and is the central long-term focus of American defense planners. China's aspirations for greater power are seen as the biggest threat to our manifold interests in East Asia. The assessment of what China can and might do with its increasing military capabilities will be a key determinant of our military posture in the region and worldwide.

China maintains that concerns about its military ambitions are exaggerated. It argues that even with recent increases its military spending is still only a small fraction of what the United States spends. There is, however, little transparency in Beijing's military spending, and Washington believes that China's actual military investment is substantially higher than the Chinese admit.

The economic dimension of our relations with China vastly complicates our ability to determine if China presents a threat or an opportunity. "Just imagine," Lee Kuan Yew once said to us, talking about China's potential power, "China will have sixty Singapores [that is, urban economic powerhouses] over the next decade." The management of our highly ramified economic relationship is itself increasingly difficult politically as American domestic concerns mount over the export of jobs to China, our huge bilateral trade deficit, Chinese attempts to purchase U.S. companies, and competition for energy supplies. When we add security threats to this volatile mix, management of the domestic political aspects of our relations with China becomes a complex exercise indeed.

True, China's ascent could be slowed or even halted by political and economic problems. But the United States cannot base its long-term policy on the possibility of China faltering. China is spending more each year to acquire greater military capabilities and the People's Liberation Army (PLA), like our own Pentagon, certainly wants more. It is prudent to assume China will continue to expand its military power, but its ability to project that power far beyond its shores will be limited for a long time. We do not know what China plans to do with its increased military capabilities, or what China's top leaders think about the purpose and utility of these capabilities, however confidently judgments on these questions are asserted in public discussion in the United States. But China's new power does confound our own strategic thinking. It also has a psychological impact on China's neighbors. At a minimum, no American administration is likely to be able politically to avoid some expensive military hedging against the growth of Chinese military power. How much hedging will be a major topic of political argument.

While China seeks a bigger stick, for the most part it speaks softly. With the exception of Taiwan, it denounces no country but rather cleverly works hard to convince countries, especially the United States, that its intentions are benign, that its growth will benefit—not threaten—the rest of the world, and that it genuinely believes in its still touted five principles of peaceful coexistence (mutual respect for sovereignty and territorial integrity, mutual nonaggression, mutual noninterference in each other's internal affairs, equality and mutual benefit, and peaceful coexistence). These principles were espoused incessantly in an earlier and different age, when China had a lot less power. Above all, China argues—not implausibly—that its continued economic success will bring even greater interdependence, which will make the cost of disruptive behavior so high that it would be effectively unthinkable. Most Asian countries have little choice but to accept Beijing's reassurance, and, as we point out in Chapter 2, "tying down Gulliver" with more reciprocal rights and obligations is a principal goal of an emerging regional consensus for greater institutionalized cooperation in East Asia.

Maintaining good relations with the United States has been the cornerstone of Chinese foreign and economic policy for many years. It still is, although many skeptical American observers see China as "buying time" for internal development. In pursuit of that policy, China has been willing from time to time to bend to the American will, even on matters that involve swallowing considerable Chinese pride and that can create domestic controversy. Avoiding fanning American fires over Taiwan has been a prime example. The minor revaluation of the Chinese yuan in mid-2005 was another tip of the hat to American politics. Nor is China completely unresponsive to official attacks on its human rights policies.

Above all the Chinese so far have been pragmatic in dealing with the United States. One senior Chinese Foreign Ministry official put it more succinctly, telling us, "You are big boys. You have deep interests in East Asia and we respect them. We do not want to compete with you for influence." These are not unreasonable sentiments, but some, perhaps many, in the Washington policy world discount them and argue that they reflect China's present situation, not its design for the future. "They are just words."

China also has worked hard to resolve problems and create friendly relations with three former rivals—India, Russia, and Vietnam. China is not just reaching out to these rivals; it sees them as part of its broader East Asia strategic framework. Its relations with Russia are perhaps the best they have been in many years, as the two even engage in significant military exercises. Beijing was instrumental in assembling the Shanghai Cooperation Organization with Russia and four Central Asian countries (Kazakhstan, Kyrgyzstan, Tajikistan, and Uzbekistan) principally to deal with security related issues in the area.

India is a particularly interesting case. The Bush administration's subordination of its concerns for the global nonproliferation regime to the goal of strengthening U.S.-India ties by sharing nuclear technology with India is a move seen by many (and heralded by American neoconservatives) as part of an effort to counter China. China has been mostly publicly silent about it, although New Delhi and Beijing have been privately talking to each other about the deal. In fact Beijing has been pursuing its own multifaceted engagement with New Delhi, exchanging senior visits, expanding its commercial relations, and increasing investments.

Chinese leaders give attention to the countries of Southeast Asia: top officials travel there frequently and, unlike our senior officials, stay more than a few hours. Beijing, of course, has a much larger stable of high-level policy officials than the United States, and they believe that in East Asia there is no substitute for personal attention. Beijing is skillfully using trade diplomacy, joint ventures, and economic and technical assistance to reassure its Southeast Asian neighbors of its benign intentions and to consolidate its position.

There is only one country with which China seems reluctant to entertain an era of good feeling—Japan. At times, it even seems Beijing goes out of its way to antagonize the Japanese, almost as if Beijing derives pleasure from poking Tokyo in the eye, a stance that seemingly makes little foreign policy sense since it drives Japan closer to the United States. The Chinese leadership also uses anti-Japanese feeling for its own domestic short-term political ends, a practice of course not unique to Beijing. Japan is not the only country at fault for troubled Sino-Japanese relations.

As for the rest of the world, China has traditionally not cared much about how other countries conduct their internal affairs as long as they do not support Taiwan independence. Beijing shows no worry about being openly associated with countries like North Korea, Burma, Sudan, and Uzbekistan—four of the world's worst states. It seems to flaunt it. Beijing has justified this policy on grounds of noninterference and pursuit of state interests. China's growing hunger for energy and other commodities has led it to areas of the Middle East, Africa, Latin America, and the South Pacific, less familiar to Beijing, where Chinese officials engage in public displays of affection with such notables as Hugo Chávez and Robert Mugabe. This is likely to become an increasingly sore point in Washington. Basically, the Chinese government's perspective has been crass, hard-headed, and self-interested, with little patience for the world's political correctness.

The United States, despite the growing polarization of American attitudes toward China, has pursued a mostly pragmatic step-by-step approach over the two decades of China's extraordinary transformation. All administrations since Nixon, wherever they started, have ended up taking, for the most part, the same conciliatory approach to China whatever the domestic political perturbations in the United States. The United States at times has been tough, at times restrained. It has not hesitated to do some things it had said it would not do, such as reinterpreting the communiqué signed with Beijing in 1982 on arms sales to Taiwan. The United States has raised high the banner of human rights and then backed off. Most important, our markets, technology, and companies have continued to contribute enormously to China's economic growth even while the United States also reaped enormous benefits.

But because of size, geography, and strategic perspectives, there will always be common and competitive interests in our bilateral relations with China regardless of how wisely or unwisely we jointly manage the relationship. China may well become more "assertive" as it becomes more powerful, even as its connectedness to the outside world will likely limit its room for maneuver. Thus, China—and a China policy—will remain, as it has been since the so-called fall of China in 1949, a football in American domestic politics. Nonetheless, we have to work out—and this obviously depends on China also— how we want to live with China's growing power and influence, in East Asia and indeed the world. This subject is now endlessly discussed in and out of government, but so far there is little agreement other than to move ahead pragmatically and seek greater contact and dialogue. The vocabulary of our internal discussion often evokes more fear than analyses, and analyses are often full of asserted assumptions about China's thirst for domination with little regard for China's many limitations.

Developing and implementing a long-term approach to our relationship with China will inevitably involve other countries in Asia, especially our closest allies, Japan and South Korea. They each have their own vital interests with China, some similar to ours but others different. China gives enormous attention to both countries. Beijing understands that Japan and Korea are important to the United States and that our policies toward them are key components of our current approach to China itself.

JAPAN

Japan is China's principal rival for influence within East Asia. It competes in many areas: for oil and gas exports from Russia, for influence and markets in Southeast Asia, and for attention on the world stage. In recent years its diplomatic relations have steadily worsened. China has refused to welcome Prime Minister Junichiro Koizumi to Beijing for over four years, and it torpedoed Japan's bid for a permanent seat on the UN Security Council. Tokyo finds it hard to accept that China is a potential superpower.

Competition can be healthy. But in this case competition is distorted by history and nationalism and can easily turn to popular animosity and confrontation. Memories of the Japanese invasion in the thirties, the subsequent harsh occupation, and World War II are still prominently recalled in China. School textbooks draw grim portraits of the Japanese. China faults Japanese textbooks as having effectively retrogressed from even the mild language explaining Japan's responsibilities for the events of the thirties and forties. One Chinese scholar put it to us this way: "If Japan cannot deal with its past, how can they manage the future?"

The most clamor is over Koizumi's insistence on visiting the Yasukuni Shrine, which he defends as a need to honor Japan's war dead. For the rest of Asia, the shrine is a place where the deeds of Class A war criminals are memorialized. Visits there by Japan's leaders are an act of contempt. The whole Yasukuni complex is in fact a tribute to prewar Japanese imperialism.

In Japan sentiment is divided. Many agree with Koizumi that the shrine is a monument of respect for Japanese who died in Japan's wars. There is also a feeling that the Chinese are using the issue to keep their own populace stirred up and to score psychological and political points. Many officials fear that acceding to Chinese demands on Yasukuni will lead to others. But many Japanese also believe the prime minister's visits are politically self-indulgent and should not have been allowed to become such a major emotional issue with Japan's neighbors. Very importantly, two of Japan's leading newspapers have mounted a frontal attack on Koizumi over his visits to Yasukuni. The issue has become a major controversy in Japan and achieving a consensus will not be easy.

However strained the official relationship, economic ties have mushroomed. Japan's trade with China is now larger than its trade with the United States, and surging exports to China have helped Japan emerge from a decade of recession. Japanese firms have heavily invested in China, and Japanese businessmen see China as an opportunity, not just a competitive challenge. With the rest of East Asia, Japan has acquired an enormous stake in China's continued success. Japanese businessmen invariably told us in no uncertain terms that the country's troubles with China were Koizumi's doing and that he ought to stop inflaming the relationship. "Hot economics, cold politics" is the usual expression in Japan to describe the situation. We would not preclude Japanese-Chinese economic dynamism bringing about a significant warming of relations once Koizumi goes in 2006.

Our alliance with Japan is a key one, and Japan has been an excellent partner. It is our principal military anchor point in East Asia, housing over half the one hundred thousand American troops in the region. American bases in Japan are essential to our ability to deal with contingencies in the Taiwan Strait or on the Korean Peninsula. Indeed, depending on what happens in South Korea, Japan could become the only place in East Asia where the United States will be able to maintain substantial American forces.

Japanese-American relations have improved during the Bush administration, in part because of Japan's growing distrust of China and North Korea. Much has also been made of the contribution of the strong personal relationship between Bush and Koizumi. The United States has given priority in East Asia to its Japan connection and has supported the expansion of Japan's security role and capabilties. Slowly but inexorably, Japan has moved to do almost everything the United States has urged in security matters. Japan has worked closely and consistently with the United States on the North Korean nuclear issue, certainly more supportively than other participants in the Six-Party effort. It is also sharing the financial burden of producing high-cost, advanced American weapons, including the development of missile defenses.

Formally, Japan's national security doctrine and its use of its military forces continue to be constrained by its constitution and by pacifist sentiments in Japan. In reality, Japan gradually but steadily has redefined its national security doctrine and funded a major increase in military capabilities; it has the fourth largest defense budget in the world. In its most dramatic gesture, Tokyo sent forces to Iraq—albeit in a noncombat role—despite popular hostility in Japan to the American attack on Iraq. The Japanese electorate well understood that their government's dispatch of troops was a gesture of support to the United States, an investment in the future of the alliance.

Strengthening the U.S.-Japan alliance and making Japan a bigger player in regional security matters, not surprisingly, have been received warily in China and South Korea. Indeed, former South Korean President Kim Dae Jung bluntly told us that he was more worried by Japan's defense buildup than by China's and that he feared the resurgence of Japanese militarism. No matter how much the United States tries to tell Beijing that our strengthened relations with Japan are not aimed at them per se, the specter of an American-sponsored effort to contain China is a prism through which China may well evaluate our policy. It is also the goal of some in the administration, and in truth our signals on Japan are confusing. They might, but so far have not, caused China to reconsider its unimpressive management of its relations with Japan.

Japanese officials, and also American ones, talk in terms of Japan becoming a "normal nation," no longer bound by the strictures of the past. There is much discussion in Japan about the constitution being formally amended to remove the formal constraints on Japan's ability to defend itself, but that still seems to be some way off. The first part of Article 9, renouncing the right to wage war, will likely remain unchanged. By the time any constitutional revision does occur, it may be a nonevent since Japan's defense policy, except the rejection of a nuclear capability, has already changed substantially.

The overall U.S.-Japan relationship has been bolstered by the constructive role Japan plays around the world, a role unequaled by far by any country in East Asia. Unfortunately, Japan gets little credit for its internationalism except in Washington. China, a huge recipient of Japanese aid for many years, shows little memory or appreciation and tends to regard Japanese aid as inadequate reparations. Many countries of Southeast Asia apparently feel the same, despite Japan's continuing assistance to the area.

Notwithstanding the growth of Japanese nationalism in recent times and all the talk about changing the "peace" constitution and even breaking the nuclear taboo, the country's broad relationship with the United States and the continued existence of an American security umbrella enable the Japanese government to continue on a cautious, generally constructive, approach to East Asia. The American alliance also gives Japan a publicly acceptable alternative to becoming a nuclear weapons state despite a growing nuclear and missile threat from North Korea. Even China acknowledges that connection. From a technical point of view, Japan could make nuclear weapons quickly, but most Japanese instinctively oppose such a course. Not only do memories of Hiroshima and Nagasaki linger, but the Japanese also realize that a decision to become a nuclear weapons power would make them a pariah in East Asia. The United States would likely oppose it, and all of East Asia would unite in condemnation.

Japan has always been sensitive to what happens in U.S.-China relations—probably never more so than when it learned of the secret Kissinger visit to China thirty odd years ago. It likes to be in close step with the Americans on foreign and security policy. Yet, Japan also wants the Sino-American relationship to be stable and not a source of enormous tension or political controversy in Japan. As one prominent Japanese ambassador succinctly put it: "Please don't force us to choose sides." That, however, is not the only perspective in Japan.

In fact, Japan has chosen sides, and every country in the region, including China, knows it. The question is how far does Tokyo go. Japan has shown an increasing willingness to talk publicly about its regional security concerns, including its interest in Taiwan's security. This new daring in Japanese rhetoric has not gone unnoticed in Beijing. On the other hand, the Japanese parse every Washington pronouncement about China. They worry about too much tension in the Beijing-Washington relationship; they worry about an overly warm Sino-American embrace that could somehow diminish U.S. ties to Japan. The bottom line is that just as the United States must take China into account as it formulates policy toward Japan, so it must factor Japan into its strategy toward China.

In Japan, as is the case with most of our democratic friends, domestic politics always can become a problematic factor in relations. With its economy finally growing again, Japan is likely to reassert itself to some degree. The long anticipated end of the Liberal Democratic Party (LDP) rule has not yet arrived. Koizumi is still in charge and remains strong and defiant, but his days are numbered. Japanese politics seem headed toward a serious two-party system in which the LDP could at times find itself in the opposition. The once powerful American-oriented Japanese bureaucracy has been shown to be neither all knowing nor all effective and occasionally even a little corrupt. Politicians have become increasingly determined to get involved in the mysteries of foreign policy. Moreover, the intellectual cliques on Japanese foreign policy have proliferated outside the foreign policy establishment and often hold sharply different views than the bureaucracy. Public diplomacy will become more important for us in Japan.

After all is said and done, Japan is a prudent power. While the public is growing tired of Chinese hectoring and anti-Japanese demonstrations in Chinese cities, Japan can be expected to carry on a generally constructive approach to China. Economic relations will expand as more Japanese companies shift production to China even as they open new facilities in Japan to produce high-quality "made in Japan" luxury goods for a growing high-end market in China. Economic ties could come to be viewed in Japan as something of a double-edged sword given Japanese fears of Chinese domination. But Japan also recognizes the increasing importance of its ties to East Asia, and especially to China. Insufficient attention is paid to Japan's robust interdependence by outsiders. We do not rule out, but at the same time do not take for granted, an inevitable trend downward in Sino-Japanese relations, even though neither country really wants it.

SOUTH KOREA

Over the past decade, South Korea has become a more complex and difficult partner for the United States. The generation that ran the country after the Korean War has faded away. The military has vanished from politics. The ideological balance between "conservatives" and "progressives" has tilted in recent years toward the progressives, who are less committed to U.S. positions. The United States is judged harshly by many Koreans who came to maturity in the seventies and eighties convinced that the United States supported authoritarian military rule. The new generation cannot be pushed about. It is proud of the country's modernization, democratization, and power.

The previous chapter discussed the sharp differences between the United States and South Korea over how to deal with the North, particularly on the nuclear issue. These differences will continue to test Washington's patience with Seoul (and vice-versa). In fact, since the beginning of the alliance, Americans and Koreans have had some bruising battles: knockdown, drag out arguments over the U.S. military presence, how to deal with North Korea, the balance between political stability and democracy, and later, trade and other economic issues. Because of South Korea's dependence on the United States, South Koreans perceived—correctly—that a disproportionate number of disputes were ultimately settled on American terms.

Anti-American feelings in South Korea have always been present, but a major increase has taken place over the past decade. One recent poll even showed that a majority of South Koreans actively believe that the United States is a greater threat to peace on the peninsula than North Korea. None of this endangers the alliance at least as long as the majority of South Koreans also believe the American presence is a necessary deterrent to Northern adventurism. But anti-American sentiment and South Korean nationalism make achieving agreement on important matters more difficult than in the past, and it erodes support for South Korea in the United States.

The aggressive pursuit of the Sunshine Policy has not thawed North Korea much, but it has given South Koreans more insight into the true condition of their cousins in the North and more confidence about dealing with them. When they look at the North they now see a pathetic land, an object of international charity, not an acute threat to their own security, but a state out of kilter with the world. Their own economic success has given them more to lose and has made them much more risk-averse in dealing with the North, further straining relations with Washington. Some American liberals and conservatives are in shock and have begun to question whether South Korea is still an ally. Such are the unexpected fruits of democracy promotion in East Asia.

Unification has always been a proclaimed goal for the South. But now as the North's economic weakness may in fact make some form of unification more possible in the not so distant future, the

South seems to prefer that unification remain a long-term prospect, after there has been some serious economic growth in the North and the political and economic costs of unification would be less. Two successive South Korean governments have carried on a concerted policy looking not toward unification but toward reconciliation with the North, despite domestic political criticisms and nasty looks from the United States. The result of the South Korean approach has been a lessening of tensions with the North but an increase of ones with the United States. South Korean public opinion is famously volatile, but government policy on North Korea both leads and reflects popular views on the costs and benefits of reconciliation and unification, respectively. We doubt this policy will change, but it surely will be tested if the Six-Party talks fail.

If peaceful unification is to become a reality, South Korea also has to bring along its two big neighbors, with which it has had, to say the least, complicated relations. Neither China nor Japan is much interested in unification. Seoul's relations with Tokyo often seem to fluctuate dramatically, but deep animosities exist, despite the impressive economic ties. Japan's influence in Korea is limited. Once violent enemies, South Korea and China have a growing array of common interests, including the continued integration of East Asia's economies and a shared approach to the North.

South Korea will seek to maintain its freedom of movement from both its larger neighbors. The nationalist Koreans are sensitive to any hint of bowing to the wishes of their bigger neighbors, and it is likely that frictions will erupt from time to time with both countries. Animosity to Japan still abounds in both Koreas. While South Korea and China have ostensibly become fast friends, Koreans also bitterly complained to us about the "dictatorial manners" and overbearing attitude of the Chinese, and both countries remember all too well their "historical differences" with each other. One veteran South Korean foreign policy pundit opined, not entirely jokingly, that at some point it will be possible that Korea will again—as in the distant past—need China's approval for the appointment of a prime minister. Whatever the snide comments, the South Korean relationship with China will grow significantly.

In this growing uncertain context, the United States still remains very important to Seoul. Caught between two bigger powers, many Koreans would like to maintain a strong American tie even after the threat from the North fades, or so many Koreans are quick to reassure Americans. The issue is the nature of those ties. While this question right now seems far off for both the South and the United States, it is an issue that gets people talking and is a particularly favored topic among officials and think tankers. In its crudest form, the question is whether Koreans want an alliance with the United States and/or a military presence or neither after some form of Korean unification. Would they want to keep American forces on the peninsula in the face of likely unhappiness on the part of China, with whom they now have a much better and more important relationship? This issue is emerging in nascent form as South Korea seeks operational command and control of the U.S.-Korean Combined Forces Command.

The recent launch of negotiations for a U.S.–South Korea FTA is both a recognition of our mutual interest in the economic relationship and a recognition of the need to strengthen the foundation of our long-term strategies. Whether these negotiations can be successfully concluded remains to be seen given the likely economic and political obstacles.

For the United States, a continued alliance with Korea in a post-unification world may make it easier to keep forces there—presumably to hedge against contingencies related to China, perhaps in the Taiwan Strait, or for broader worldwide purposes. If that is our long-term goal, we had better start working toward it now. That would not go down well in Beijing, but it seems unlikely that China would do more than complain. We personally find it hard to believe that the highly nationalist Koreans would want American troops around after unification. But that will depend in part on what is happening elsewhere in East Asia and in the world. Some Americans, particularly but not only in the Pentagon, think U.S. military forces are wonderful and every country including Korea should have some of them.

In general, South Korea tends to be underestimated in East Asia. It is an enormously dynamic country, one of the fast movers and shakers in our digital age and is rapidly expanding its international reach. It is now generating its own scientific and technical innovations. Its major companies compete head-to-head—and successfully—with their Japanese and American counterparts. Koreans see China as their backyard for turning out new electronic products as well as a growing market. Seoul is playing an active role in building

East Asian regional institutions and has argued for enhanced regional cooperation and the ultimate creation of an East Asian Community based on ASEAN Plus Three—that is, without the involvement of the United States. It also aspires to a larger role in the world, including putting its current foreign minister into Kofi Annan's chair. In ten years, one thing is likely: we will see an even stronger and more internationally active South Korea—and maybe, just maybe, a unified Korea.

5

SOUTHEAST ASIA
ONCE AGAIN ON THE SCREEN

*F*our decades ago Southeast Asia was the center of American foreign policy in Asia, the linchpin in our long campaign to prevent communism from "inexorably sweeping over the region." Yet despite the incessant predictions of our leading wise men of the time, Southeast Asia did not disintegrate after South Vietnam fell and U.S. troops withdrew, nor did our influence recede. The Vietnamese occupation of Cambodia in 1979 produced a huge, indeed incredible, American humanitarian response; we took in over a million people fleeing from Laos, Cambodia, and Vietnam. Since then—whether by choice or circumstance—the United States has not exhibited overwhelming concern about the region, and Southeast Asia has moved to the periphery of America's East Asian policy.

This period of benign detachment may be coming to an end. The events of September 11 and our discovery of Islamic extremism in the region renewed our engagement in the area, elevating Southeast Asia to a "second front" in the war on terrorism. Also prodding our thinking about the region is the sense that China's growing presence and influence there threatens American interests. Indeed, during our visits to Southeast Asian capitals in early 2005, we frequently heard the comment that "China was cleaning our clock" in the area, whatever that means.

Southeast Asia has changed tremendously over the past generation. Today, it is an impressive region of ten states (plus East Timor and Papua New Guinea) at different stages of development and governance, bound together in East Asia's most established regional organization, ASEAN. It is home to nearly 600 million people with a collective GDP of approximately $800 billion in 2004, growing in recent years at a highly respectable, though not dramatic, rate of 5 to 6 percent. (See Table 5.1, page 96.) American commercial interests in the region are substantial. In 2004, U.S. trade with ASEAN countries reached some $136 billion, making it our fifth largest trading partner, and U.S. direct investment in the region totaled some $90 billion.

Of greater interest to Americans now than previously is that 40 percent of the region's populace is Muslim. (The rest are mostly Buddhist or Christian.) Its largest country, Indonesia, is the world's biggest Muslim nation by a considerable margin and an infant democracy to boot. Pockets of Islamic extremism in the area are still small but continue to produce serious acts of violence in some countries. Moreover, there is evidence of regional terrorist networks operating across national boundaries.

Geography has not changed, and the geostrategic importance of the region is undiminished. Twenty-five percent of the world's shipping, including approximately half the world's oil and gas trade, passes through Southeast Asia's narrow sea lanes each year. Its vulnerability to piracy draws international attention. It is also the center of messy territorial disputes involving a goodly number of East Asian countries. With the rising U.S. military emphasis on greater flexibility and mobility, access to Southeast Asian ports has become—as during the cold war—important to America's global and regional security posture.

While the collective importance of Southeast Asia is greater than its national parts, over the past decade "Southeast Asia" as a whole has drawn American attention mostly—often belatedly—in times of crisis. Southeast Asians still complain heatedly that America's initial lack of attention added to the severity of the financial crisis of the late nineties. Only after September 11 did the United States acknowledge the combustible symbiosis between Islamic extremism and weak states in the area. We quickly stepped up counterterrorism cooperation with nearly all Southeast Asian governments. On the other hand, our emphasis on strengthening governance in the region, supposedly a basic element of rooting out terrorism, appears more talk than action.

It was the terrible tsunami in December 2004 that briefly reawakened American public attention to the region. The United States responded impressively officially—and with a massive outpouring of private aid as well. U.S. officials were heartened when humanitarian relief efforts—delivered in great part by the American military—received rave reviews in the area. "We're on a high" was the refrain from senior U.S. officials in the region with whom we met just days after the tsunami. The demonstration of U.S. willingness to translate its "hard power" into humanitarian assistance and compassion was a short-term boon that reversed declining perceptions in Southeast Asia of America and its priorities in the region. Not surprisingly, American public interest declined as memories of the tsunami faded and our own calamities—manmade and natural—became the focus of media attention.

Notwithstanding our responses to the region's crises, the United States pursues a set of primarily bilateral policies in its dealings with Southeast Asian countries. Recent American efforts to put more content into its relationships in the area have been spasmodic: some counterterrorism support here, a bit of development financing there, an occasional, always brief presidential visit, frequent statements affirming commitments to enhance U.S.-ASEAN relations, and declaratory support to proliferating multilateralism in the area.

Part of our difficulty in moving beyond a bilateral fixation in the region is that Southeast Asia is such a heterogeneous area. In addition to the sheer diversity of its people, the region's countries are at different stages of economic development and political transition—some still quite fragile. (See Table 5.1, page 96.) Thailand, for example, is light years ahead of neighboring Laos. Often language gets in the way of communication. These dichotomies work against regional cohesion, and privately Southeast Asian officials will be the first to state this fact. ASEAN—a central point of engagement for governments outside the area—is aware of the "development gap," as they call it, but does little about it.

ASEAN remains a two-tiered structure whose members give primacy to the principle of "noninterference" in one another's internal affairs. Instead of focusing on narrowing the economic divides and building state capacity among its members, the organization has substituted clever branding ("Unity in Diversity" or "One Vision, One Identity, One Community") and relies on a proliferation of meetings, initiatives, declarations, and collective visions all aimed at engendering greater political cooperation. It has not tried to put together resources, institutional wherewithal, and a conceptual basis to move much

TABLE 5.1. KEY INDICATORS FOR ASEAN COUNTRIES, 2004

	POPULATION (MILLION)	GDP (BILLION)	GDP PER CAPITA	GDP GROWTH (%)	FDI, NET INFLOWS (MILLION)	DEBT (BILLION)	GOVERNMENT TYPE	UNDP HUMAN DEVELOPMENT INDEX HDI VALUE	HDI RANK*
Singapore	4.34	106.82	23,636.04	8.41	11,430.80	—	Parliamentary Republic	0.907	25
Brunei	0.36	5.18	13,879.00	4.00	—	—	Constitutional Sultanate	0.866	33
Malaysia	25.21	117.78	4,220.63	7.06	2,473.16	49.07	Constitutional Monarchy	0.796	61
Thailand	62.39	163.49	2,399.36	6.05	1,949.27	51.79	Constitutional Monarchy	0.778	73
Philippines	82.99	86.43	1,079.32	6.15	319.00	62.66	Republic	0.758	84
Indonesia	217.59	257.64	906.19	5.13	-596.92	134.39	Republic	0.697	110
Vietnam	82.16	45.21	500.49	7.50	1,450.00	15.82	Communist State	0.704	108
Laos	5.79	2.41	371.50	6.00	19.48	2.85	Communist State	0.545	133
Cambodia	13.63	4.60	327.84	6.00	86.96	3.14	Constitutional Monarchy	0.571	130
Burma	49.91	9.08	166.00	5.00	133.51	7.32	Military Junta	0.578	129

Note: Figures for FDI and debt use 2003 data. All amounts in current U.S. dollars, except GDP per capita, which uses constant 2000 U.S. dollars.
* Rank is out of 177 countries surveyed

Source: World Bank, *World Bank Development Indicators, 2005.*
UNDP, *Human Development Report, 2005,* available online at http://hdr.undp.org/reports/global/2005/.
GDP data for Brunei and Burma taken from ASEAN, *Statistical Yearbook, 2005,* available online at http://www.aseansec.org/18175.htm.
Political system classification from CIA *World Factbook,* available online at http://www.cia.gov/cia/publications/factbook/.

beyond rhetoric, and real progress has been elusive. The founding ASEAN nations (Thailand, Indonesia, Singapore, Malaysia, and the Philippines) find it more congenial to consort with their Western friends in a variety of forums, high and low, than to invest the political energy and capital to help build a greater commonality of interest and perspective among themselves and the new entrants. Nearly forty years after its creation, there is still no real sense of an ASEAN community except among a small fraternity of officials and scholars who make their living off of it. As an institution, ASEAN makes its decisions on the basis of consensus and has no ability to enforce implementation of agreed upon measures. This is recognized, and some ASEAN countries are searching for ways to enhance ASEAN's relevance.

To be fair, ASEAN has produced some positive, important results besides its dealings with countries outside the area. It has reduced tensions among its members, helped reverse the Vietnamese occupation of Cambodia in the eighties, and created a small, but useful and growing, web of economic and security cooperation. It has provided the cornerstone for wider East Asian economic cooperation with China, Japan, and South Korea, the so-called ASEAN Plus Three (APT), and a center for multilateral security consultations in the ASEAN Regional Forum (ARF). Despite all the hype devoted to ASEAN by its member countries, most states remain focused on their own internal problems and bilateral relations with immediate neighbors. ASEAN does not pose a challenge to America's bilateral approach. While officialdom gives due lip service to ASEAN, the United States does not really do much concretely with the institution. Nor, in truth, do we really expect much from it.

WHAT'S ON U.S. MINDS IN SOUTHEAST ASIA

CHINA'S LOOMING SHADOW

Today's talk in Washington (and in Southeast Asia for that matter) about Southeast Asia usually ends up in conversations about China's growing reach into its southern hinterland. Indeed, the ultimate driver of U.S. thinking about Southeast Asia and its policies toward the region may turn out to be not so much what is happening within the region itself but rather from without—that is, China.

China's looming presence is generating new realities in Southeast Asia. The once reliable notion that the United States is the external guarantor of regional stability is now questioned. Regional economic growth, political stability, and interstate security now hinge on a more complex set of factors. The U.S. economy, as well as its military presence, are certainly among them. It was the U.S. military after all, not China's PLA, that was able to send ships into the Indian Ocean to respond to the 2004 tsunami crisis. But cultivation of an American military presence is no longer a priority of governments in the region. They also must manage an ever-deeper integration with the Chinese economy while many are under continuing pressures to establish better governance and a stronger association among themselves.

In fact, Southeast Asian countries have been adjusting to the growing economic and political weight of China for the past decade: they have had no choice. To be pro-China is no longer the diplomatic no-no that it once was in Southeast Asian capitals. To the contrary, Chinese businessmen, Chinese goods, and Chinese tourists are ever-present throughout the region. As a well-weathered and influential Thai government adviser observed of China: "In Southeast Asia it is like the air you breathe. It's all around you and you have to deal with them." Thai businessmen no longer hide their Chinese roots while doing business in their neighborhoods.

This does not mean, of course, that the air is equally pure in every Southeast Asian country. China is still distrusted, notably in Indonesia and Vietnam. One Vietnamese scholar cautioned, "When you live with a giant you don't know when it will be a threat." Perhaps true, but predictions and assumptions about China's geopolitical ambitions in Southeast Asia vary. Elites look to China's generally prudent behavior in the rest of Asia, in the Taiwan Strait and North Korea in particular, and put their minds more at ease. Some countries—like Thailand and to a lesser degree Malaysia—seem to be quite comfortable living in China's pocket. Some mischievous Thais even use the term "lackey" to characterize the Thai government's relations with Beijing. On the other hand, almost all countries of the region have a strong sense of national identity and will be vigilant in asserting and protecting their independence from any excess of Chinese pressures. Economic ties with Beijing have flourished far more than security-related cooperation except for Burma.

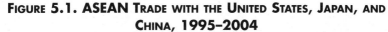

FIGURE 5.1. ASEAN TRADE WITH THE UNITED STATES, JAPAN, AND CHINA, 1995–2004

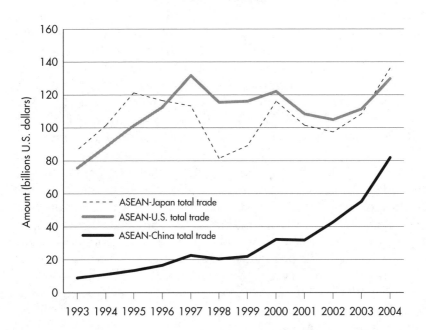

Source: ASEAN, *Statistical Yearbook, 2005,* available online at http://www.aseansec.org /18175.htm.

The ASEAN countries trade and investment flows with China are booming. The Chinese government reported that trade in 2004 rose 35.3 percent from 2003 to more than $100 billion on top of an astounding 42.8 percent increase the year before. U.S.-ASEAN trade has hardly doubled over the last decade. (See Figure 5.1.) China is moving quickly to capitalize on this integration. It is reducing tariffs on Southeast Asian goods and hopes to finalize an FTA with the original five ASEAN members in 2010 and the remaining members by 2015. China's move triggered a series of FTA negotiations between ASEAN and Asia's other big powers, Japan, South Korea, and India. For its part, the United States has barely worked out an arrangement for a U.S.-ASEAN Summit in the near future, possibly in 2007, and the bilateral FTA is still our vehicle of choice for building economic ties in the area—although only one has been concluded at this point.

For Southeast Asia, China's economic success is of course a double-edged sword. Southeast Asians reap significant benefits, but they fear Chinese competition and dread a "hollowing out" of their manufacturing sectors and loss of jobs as a result. Southeast Asian leaders and business executives are also concerned that China's enormous attraction for foreign direct investment will reduce flows into their economies. Alert to negative perceptions, Beijing has promised to increase its own investment in Southeast Asian countries; in its 2005 agreement with Indonesia, Beijing undertook to invest between $10–20 billion in Indonesia by 2010. Whether those increases actually occur remains to be seen. Other problems arise for Southeast Asia from China's economic advance. For example, China's increasing demand for the region's natural resources has serious environmental consequences that governments have difficulty in addressing.

China uses access to its markets to consolidate its relationships in the region and reassure the neighborhood that its geopolitical ambitions are benign. The principle of "mutual benefit" has become something of a new diplomatic mantra for Chinese statecraft in Southeast Asia. High-level Chinese delegations shuttle from capital to capital, listening to local concerns, portraying China as a fellow developing nation, and never missing the opportunity to point out that China's success redounds to the benefit of Southeast Asia and vice versa. This line of approach seems to be working. Southeast Asian leaders have themselves adopted what some call a "win-win" formulation of creating deeper economic and political ties with China.

The process has been gradual and Chinese diplomacy has been cautious. Throughout the nineties, Beijing invested heavily in bilateral relations and negotiated strategic cooperation agreements with each Southeast Asian country, despite bilateral flare-ups such as the clash with the Philippines in 1995 over ownership of Mischief Reef in the South China Sea. Recently, Beijing has shown a growing affinity for multilateralism and cultivated further its ties with the region through increased participation with ASEAN, ARF, and the Greater Mekong Subregion program, an effort initiated by the Asian Development Bank to increase social and economic development among the six countries (Cambodia, Laos, Vietnam, Thailand, Burma, and China) along the Mekong River.

China's model for development—itself—has resonated with many neighbors. China admits, even embraces publicly, its own internal challenges while it trumpets its accomplishments. China's tone is quite different from Japan's. The difference is one between the present and the past, between developing and developed. China says we are going through this now, together, let's help each other. Japan says we've been there, simply follow our example, learn from our mistakes, and one day you too can be where we are now. In February 2005, Singapore's Senior Minister Goh Chok Tong declared, perhaps a bit too fulsomely, "China's extraordinary development sets the example for other Asian countries to follow and thus drives Asia's transformation." And yet while Japan's investment and aid to Southeast Asian countries far outweighs China's, it does not generate the same reception or influence in the region: Chinese assistance, especially to its immediate neighbors, Burma, Laos, and Cambodia, wins far greater attention.

In Southeast Asian minds, the road is, hopefully, not just one-way to China. ASEAN has sought to use China's commitment to peaceful integration to further involve China in its regional infrastructure. At the 2003 ASEAN Summit in Bali, China acceded to the Treaty of Amity and Cooperation (TAC)—the pillar of ASEAN's commitment to the peaceful resolution of disputes—and signed the Joint Declaration on Strategic Partnership for Peace and Prosperity, which outlines cooperation on economic development and security. China is an ardent devotee of ASEAN's guiding principle of noninterference and has begun to align its security outlook with countries in the region. In a speech in 2004, President Hu Jintao elaborated China's position on security in Southeast Asia: "[China] will give full play to existing multilateral security mechanisms and is ready to set up a security dialogue mechanism with other Asian countries to actively promote confidence-building in the military field." Rhetoric or not, it gets good play.

China's good neighbor approach gets a bit frayed when the generalities and rhetoric of regional cooperation bump up against basic national interests. The continuing disputes over the South China Sea are a good example. Conflicting claims to resources, especially petroleum and natural gas, in the South China Sea among China, the Philippines, Vietnam, Malaysia, Brunei, and Taiwan have produced some serious abrasions. The Declaration on the Conduct of Parties in the South China Sea signed by China and ASEAN in 2002 was a seeming start toward cooperative resolution of this difficult issue, but it has remained just that—a declaration and not the *code* of conduct ASEAN seeks. (A desired code is currently in the works.) China reverted to a bilateral approach with the Philippines and, in September 2004, concluded a "joint-development" agreement for territory under dispute that allows for the joint collection and exchange of seismic data. Vietnam predictably was not pleased and argued that China's notion of joint development was merely a de facto extension of Chinese sovereignty. It was months before Vietnam worked out a trilateral arrangement to participate in joint development, but any possibility of joint-resource extraction is still a long way off. Quiet for the moment, differences over the South China Sea will likely continue to produce periodic strains in ASEAN-China relations.

Whatever their national sensitivities to a resurgent China, the economic destinies of the neighboring nations are intertwined with China's. Southeast Asians understand this fully. China's demand for Southeast Asian raw materials and agricultural products is growing exponentially. As its hunger for oil rises sharply, China becomes more interested in Southeast Asian countries. Chinese diplomacy has been adept and its "practicality" in providing aid and financial commitments is more encouraging to Southeast Asian governments than "fussy" Japanese bureaucratic requirements. In a sense, much of Southeast Asia has become an important part of the greater Chinese economy.

ISLAM AND TERRORISM

Prior to September 11, the U.S. government viewed terrorism in Southeast Asia primarily as a domestic problem, and for the most part left Southeast Asian governments to deal with it, even though it long recognized that Islamic fundamentalism might become a serious challenge to governance in Indonesia and Malaysia. Sporadic outbreaks of violence in Muslim areas of Thailand and the Philippines and the threat they posed to national economies and regional stability also concerned us. But, on balance, except for cases in which there were clear links back to Southeast Asia, as with the first plot against the World Trade Center in 1993, the United States was not much engaged. The events of September 11 greatly heightened American attention to the threat of international terrorism directed against citizens of the United States abroad and our friends. The U.S. government felt the need for more intelligence and understanding of the role of Islam in Southeast Asia and more specifically on Islamic extremism, communal violence, and the connection to international terrorism.

Terrorism is, of course, all too familiar to the governments and peoples of Southeast Asia; it is America's involvement in the effort to eradicate it that is new. American single-mindedness on terrorism has presented Southeast Asian governments, especially those with majority Muslim populations, with a difficult balancing act, involving managing their relations with the United States with its persistent importuning on counterterrorism and at the same time addressing popular dissatisfaction with American policy. This task has become more complicated, perhaps temporarily, as Muslims in the region have focused on American policy in the broader Muslim world. The wars in Afghanistan and Iraq aroused animosity toward the United States among Muslims in Southeast Asia, and the United States is often portrayed as pursuing a global "crusade" against Islam. Similarly, the American position on Israeli-Palestinian issues, more than in the past, has aroused greater anger in the region.

Southeast Asia is home to approximately 250 million Muslims. Three countries—Indonesia, Malaysia, and Brunei—have majority Muslim populations, and the first two have small but serious radical elements. Two others—Thailand and the Philippines—have sizable minority Muslim populations, mostly concentrated in areas with long-standing separatist insurgencies. Radical groups have the capability to challenge the central government and disrupt public order. Some Muslim insurgents in the Philippines have connections with outside jihadist networks, receiving financial support from them and providing training grounds for them.

Islam's role in the region and its politics are complex and do not play to our strong suits. Muslims in these countries are grappling with questions regarding Islam's role in national life and governance. As one scholar counseled us, "On Islam and politics I do not think one can distinguish between the two. The question is how will the people interpret their faith in the public square?"

Scholars tend to agree that Muslims in Southeast Asia tend to be "moderate" with vast diversity in practice. In Indonesia and Malaysia, Islam deeply informs national identity and domestic politics. For many Muslim Indonesians, there is no discontinuity between the values of their faith and the practice of their democracy. Many tend to avoid the word secular and seek to strengthen a modern democratic state infused by religion. In fact, Muslim leaders suggested to us that Indonesia's two largest mass-based Muslim organizations—Muhammadiyah and Nahdlatul Ulama (NU)—have been critical to the development of a culture of democracy in the country. These organizations have gone to some lengths to articulate how democratic values are rooted in Islam, and they have engaged in civic education at the grassroots level in the post-Suharto era. While Islamic political parties have increased their participation in Indonesia's government in the past two parliamentary elections, Islamist politicking has been tempered by growing public demands for cleaning up the government and delivering public goods, not for enshrining *sharia*, the religious law of Islam, into state law. Not all view the situation as so benign; many see Islamist groups seeking political power as well as the growth of a stricter Islamic consciousness and culture in the country.

That is not to say that violent Islamic extremism does not threaten Indonesia's fragile political transition and the government's ability to cultivate a climate of security, law, and order conducive to foreign investment and tourism. Jemaah Islamiyah (JI)—a militant Islamist group operating in Southeast Asia with links to al Qaeda and responsible for various attacks, including the devastating Bali bombings in 2002—is still a serious security concern in Indonesia and predictions of its demise are premature, although its ability to carry out attacks seems to be waning. Sorting out JI from regional Islamist networks, local jihadists, and those involved primarily in sectarian conflicts in the archipelago is also becoming an increasingly murky exercise. Indonesia's government, led by former president Megawati Sukarnoputri, was late to grasp the reality of terrorism, and became aroused only after the 2002 Bali bombings and subsequent bombings in Jakarta in 2003 at the Marriott Hotel and in 2004 at the Australian embassy. Similar reservations about the awareness of the current administration of Susilo Bambang Yudhoyono were expressed after the more recent Bali bombings in 2005.

Radical religious groups are seeking to expand their political reach at local levels by taking advantage of Indonesia's accelerated effort to devolve political power to the provincial and municipal levels. An avid Indonesia watcher observed that radical Islam "is no longer a Jakarta-centered thing [but has moved] to where local politicians pander to Islamist groups." In general, Western observers of

Indonesia still seem frustrated at what they find to be a lack of government toughness in the counterterrorism campaign and too much interference from politicians worrying about political support.

In the Philippines—and to a much lesser degree in Thailand—Islamic extremism has become entrenched in local separatist conflicts that have defied resolution for decades. For nearly forty years, the Philippine government has contended with an insurgency in its southern island of Mindanao where Moro Muslims are heavily interspersed with non-Muslims. Some Americans and many Filipinos have seen the problem more as one of systematic banditry than religious extremism. After September 11, greater scrutiny from both Manila and Washington uncovered linkages between Islamic separatist groups, such as the Moro Islamic Liberation Front (MILF) and the more radical but much smaller Abu Sayyaf Group, with external terrorist organizations, including JI and al Qaeda.

The initial American reaction was to make Mindanao a significant point of engagement in the global war on terrorism. For the Philippine government, Mindanao is mainly a worrying source of internal instability. Manila has welcomed an increase in U.S. economic and military assistance in return for antiterrorism collaboration. The roots of the problem lie in long-standing Muslim grievances about control of their "ancestral domain" as well as lack of government follow-through on granting greater administrative autonomy and providing more funding for education and other public services. These grievances plus the "nothing-to-lose" mentality of many young Filipino Muslims create fertile ground for violent extremists, including those from outside the Philippines.

For nearly the past decade, the government and the MILF have sporadically pursued a peace process, brokered since 2003 by Malaysia and interspersed by fighting and intermittent ceasefires. The links between international terrorist organizations and the domestic insurgency has complicated the peace process. The MILF leadership has disavowed terrorism, but many believe the MILF still has links to the ongoing terrorist activity. While a peace deal supposedly is on the horizon, the terrorist problem is not likely to go away soon and challenges the central government's ability to deal with the underlying causes of the problem.

Thailand's three southern provinces, home to the majority of Thailand's minority Malay Muslim population, have long been a source of intermittent low-grade pain for the Thai government. Bangkok has never managed to resolve the persistent social and economic grievances of its Muslim population completely, but Thai governments have usually been able to address specific tensions as they arose and prevent serious violence, that is until recently. For the administration of Thaksin Shinawatra, the separatist insurgency in the South has become more like an acute infection.

Thaksin has moved from denying the existence of terrorist activities and rising discontent among the nation's Muslim population to sounding alarms about the spread of terrorism. He proceeded to carry out a heavy-handed military crackdown in the South, which has entrenched old grievances and escalated tensions. Violence has increased, and some one thousand people have been killed.

Many Thai believe the Thaksin government is losing control of the situation and could face an escalation of violence that would affect economic confidence and tourism. Muslims in southern Thailand have not proclaimed jihad, but if some degree of trust is not restored, the problem could metastasize into a serious Islamic insurgency, offering opportunity for outside extremists to intervene. It has already led to a serious quarrel within ASEAN among Thailand, Malaysia, and Indonesia. And there is the danger that the problem may spill over the border with Malaysia, as Thai Muslims seek refuge there.

U.S. involvement in these matters throughout the region for the most part takes the form of support for and cooperation with local police and military, particularly to help with training and intelligence. It appears that the United States is restrained in offering advice. Quite correctly, it does not try to get involved in sorting out the complex interrelationship between Islam and the state or complicated internal conflicts in heavily Muslim countries.

WEAK STATES AND GOVERNANCE

After September 11, top American officials frequently proclaimed that the United States learned a painful lesson from "walking out" of Afghanistan after the Soviets were forced out, the lesson being that the United States must pay attention to weak and failing states that can serve as breeding grounds for terrorism, as well as drugs and

HIV/AIDS. The United States, of course, pays little or no attention to many weak and fragile states. At most, Americans look at such states in a narrowly focused, short-term context. If there are identifiable bad guys around, hatching dangerous plots or training other bad guys, we pay closer attention and perhaps increase our resources and involvement.

Southeast Asia has its share of weak states. The ones that have captured our attention have significant, if not majority, Muslim populations. The Philippines and Indonesia fall in that category. Even there, however, American efforts to address issues of security and terrorism far eclipse those to strengthen governance or build the capacity for rule of law and civil society.

Loudly proclaiming its call for democracy in the area, the United States preaches that democracy and good governance go hand in hand. That is, of course, not always true, and we focus more on the former than the latter, in many ways the easier of the two. We have left much of the task of building governmental capacity, a long-term undertaking, to international bodies and often to American NGOs funded by the U.S. government.

For Southeast Asia's burgeoning democracies like Indonesia, what will make them stronger and more stable is not just their ability to organize elections—important as that is—or even their ability to capture high-level terrorists. What will enable these countries to consolidate nascent democratic institutions are, of course, governments that can do more than make popular promises, but can infuse dynamism and confidence into their economies. Consistency is also a problem. One scholar in Jakarta said to us: "How many presidents has the United States had since George Washington? 43. Indonesia has had 6, Malaysia 5, Singapore 3. We are a very young democracy here. With young democracies you are unable to change governments every four years and maintain policy."

For Southeast Asia's least advanced states—Cambodia, Laos, and Burma—good governance let alone democracy are not high on the list of those who hold power. Each country is mired in backwardness, criminality, and an increasing HIV/AIDS epidemic. The governments are authoritarian, their people are impoverished and undereducated, and their economies are largely stagnant. Laos and increasingly Cambodia now are mostly forgotten by the American public. The small American public that is interested is far more focused on war crimes trials for past heinous deeds in Cambodia than what is going on under Prime Minister Hun Sen. Burma, the region's celebrity laggard, gets a lot of verbal abuse in the U.S. Congress and is the object of periodic editorials lamenting Rangoon's latest barbarism.

The sad part is that these three states need help badly. Equally sad is that their governments are hard to help and are unlikely to make good use of the help they receive. They also are governments with which the United States in recent years has varyingly had a contentious history, changing levels of interaction, and little political investment. In the case of Burma, legitimate disdain for its military junta has hardened us to a deepening humanitarian crisis in almost every area of human activity. The military keeps dragging the country down. Our domestic politics make it hard to provide greater humanitarian assistance, even if we knew how to do it effectively. (Burma is discussed in detail in the next chapter.)

The stronger and richer nations of the region also shoulder some blame here. They gave ASEAN membership to the other Southeast Asian countries supposedly with the intent of helping to transform them but little has been transformed. Admittedly, financial resources are limited. And yet for years, in keeping with the traditional ASEAN practice of noninterference and consensus decisionmaking, the original members have watched terrible events unfold notably, but not only, in Burma. They have mostly refused to examine or even comment on the internal affairs of these new members, let alone help them. That is standard practice for ASEAN countries—no interference in internal affairs. ASEAN members are focused on their individual problems and leave the provision of assistance for their weaker neighbors to the international community.

Additionally, in the case of Burma, effecting change in the regime runs up against the domestic priorities of its neighbor Thailand. Prime Minister Thaksin has declared that Thailand would assume the task of helping its nearest and weakest neighbors, Laos, Cambodia, and Burma. But under Thaksin that has largely meant promoting Thai investment, and supporting the Burmese military leadership and trying to pass off their token constitutional efforts as serious reform. To be fair, Bangkok is legitimately concerned with some of Burma's main exports—drugs, migrant workers, and HIV/AIDS—and apparently hoped that a conciliatory approach to the Burmese military would limit the extent to which they flowed across the Thai border. That too so far has not worked.

The discussion of weak states and governance is a favorite topic for academics and politicians in Southeast Asia, but concrete help seems far off. Human security concerns, from Avian Flu to HIV/AIDS to poverty eradication, rank higher with them than security issues such as terrorism. In the end, only governments can do much about them, and they are mostly failing.

BIG STATES: FOCUSING ON THE POWER

Whatever the importance of ASEAN or the growth of wider East Asian regional institutions, the principal relationships for the United States in the region will remain bilateral for some time to come. Four big countries are central to assuring the broad stability and independence of the area: Thailand, the Philippines, Indonesia, and Vietnam. A few words about each.

Thailand, along with the Philippines, has long been America's closest friend and ally in Southeast Asia. American investment in that relationship has paid great dividends for both countries, despite occasional ups and downs, as the coordination of America's tsunami response effort showed. As one senior U.S. diplomat rightfully pointed out regarding that effort, "And, of course, this could not have happened without fifty years of investing in the relationship!" Our economic ties are flourishing. Romance is important in bilateral relationships, but the Thais are above all realistic and pragmatic, and Thailand makes every effort to accommodate the United States on issues of importance to us, including capturing foreign terrorists.

Today, Thailand has become a politically strong, economically dynamic state growing in self-confidence. Its economic performance has been impressive. In 2004, GDP per capita reached $2,399 and total trade with the United States reached $24 billion. The Thai military is still important but has lost its political dominance. The country is a free and democratically functioning state, although there has been serious erosion of political checks and balances under Thaksin. Thaksin remains popular in rural Thailand, but his current troubles in Bangkok may be undermining his hold on power. Thailand has not traditionally been a formidable presence in Southeast Asia, although under Thaksin it has taken a more visible role in the region.

The biggest change in Thai foreign policy has been in its relations with China, which have steadily strengthened since the end of the Vietnam War and expanded impressively in the past decade. In 2004, total trade with China reached $15 billion, a decade earlier it was only $1.3 billion. Thai investment in China has been big and profitable; indeed, the biggest foreign investor in China is a Thai company. China's embassy in Bangkok is one of its biggest in the world. Thailand has to a considerable extent thrown in its lot with China, but it is too strong and too nationalistic to be simply a lackey of Beijing. It will maintain close ties with the United States, but money talks and for Thais, China is now where the bank is. Thais do not hesitate, however, to express their displeasure with China. China's "early harvest" FTA with Thailand has been immensely unpopular and is widely viewed as China taking advantage of poor Thai farmers.

U.S. ties with the Philippines remain important though they have declined in strategic value. The end of the cold war coincided with a nationalist-inspired political timetable in the Philippines aimed at bringing about the departure of American forces from the military bases at Clark and Subic.

In the late eighties and early nineties, following the departure of Ferdinand Marcos and the restoration of a democratic system, the Philippines seemed to be a beacon for democracy in the region. That beacon has dimmed as the Philippines faltered and as its neighbors, especially Thailand, have advanced politically and economically.

The DNA of one person, one vote democracy may carry a regressive gene of populism, especially in countries with great poverty, such as the Philippines. Votes can be purchased; electorates can be wooed with extensive promises, including those that are unaffordable; and politicians change alliances with alacrity. Corruption is a major problem that saps public confidence in government. Governance in the Philippines is sorely inadequate, making it difficult to meet basic needs for education and public health, which contributes to its Muslim insurgency. Despite its great resources, there is no simple solution to what ails the Philippines. Given history, our close connections, and its internal terrorist threats, the United States will not likely consign the Philippines to benign neglect. Simply paying attention may be the most important part of U.S. policy toward the Philippines.

Indonesia and Vietnam have the potential and resources to add real weight and influence to the region and to strengthen ASEAN.

Indonesia is the biggest and potentially most powerful state in the area. Since the fall of Suharto in 1998, Indonesia has had to recover from the financial disaster of the late nineties and struggle through a series of weak governments. It is not clear whether the impressive elections of 2004 mark a real turning point. Currently, Indonesia is not doing badly. Its GDP growth hovers around 5 percent, and it seems to be making progress in attracting foreign investment and providing greater human security for its people. As one Indonesia analyst observed, "There is a quiet pride of transformation in Indonesia that the government must capitalize on by improving the daily life and security of its people." That is no easy job.

The ability of the new government to produce meaningful reform, effectively manage tsunami reconstruction, and build new infrastructure is uncertain. The president is saying the right things and showing determination, but implementation is slow. He deserves kudos for helping to resolve the difficulties in Aceh, Indonesia's rebellious province that has been at war with the central government for thirty years. It is too early to know for sure whether the recently negotiated agreement with the separatists will last. Distrust persists on both sides, but progress has been impressive.

U.S.-Indonesian relations are still troubled by the past, especially by the conduct of the Indonesian military in East Timor. For many years, the United States strongly supported the authoritarian Suharto government. Increasingly agitated by massive Indonesian human rights violations in the nineties, however, Congress has proved slow to give the administration room to improve bilateral relations, particularly on ending restrictions on military assistance. The United States has recently started the process of rebuilding a relationship with the Indonesian military, which has certainly lost its dominance but not its influence. The Pentagon has resumed the military training program, which is an important complement to the ongoing U.S. training of Indonesia's police forces, and it most recently began providing hardware. The effects of a fifteen-year gap in the military-to-military relationship with the United States were evident during the tsunami crisis, when the Indonesian military was ill-prepared to work effectively with American and Australian forces in the disaster relief effort. China, unlike the

United States, reportedly has declared its readiness to provide significant military assistance to Indonesia, but that has yet to be seen.

Vietnam's eighty million people are coming out of their shell and want to be a part of the world. Despite its desperately low per capita income, the country's dynamism is palpable, and it has impressive resources and human capital. It has pursued a low posture in ASEAN and focused on its internal development.

Normalization of ties with the United States in 1995 and the end of a forty-year trade embargo helped trigger significant advances in Vietnam's economy and its relations in the region and internationally. The country's biggest problem has been the dead hand of the Communist Party, which asserts its commitment to socialism even while trying to open its economy to a globalizing world. Vietnam has proceeded with far more hesitation than China, however, obviously fearing for internal stability and the party's own dominant position. The existence of an authoritarian and repressive government has complicated efforts to enhance U.S.-Vietnam relations.

To be sure, Vietnam still shows its independence, much as it has done throughout its history. It will clearly not be a vassal state to anyone. One former high-ranking military official chose his words carefully as he conceded, "Historically when we have depended on another country and given up some of our sovereignty it has been a failure for Vietnam. Whenever we have independence there have been successes. We want to have civil relations with several powers." The collapse of the Soviet Union and the loss of its major economic assistance was a painful, though useful, lesson for Vietnam. Today, it avoids dependence on any one relationship and actively cultivates multiple relationships, bilateral and multilateral.

China remains its abiding security concern, and Vietnam approaches its neighbor with a combination of animosity and fear. Since normalizing relations with China in 1991, prudence and pragmatism have prevailed, trade has expanded, and relations have improved. Ironically, Vietnam may also be the most pro-American country in the area, seeing it as the major security balance against China. Preoccupied with other matters, including terrorism and China, however, the United States has been treating Vietnam as almost a minor matter. There are signs that is changing. A presidential visit will help.

◆ ◆ ◆

For the United States, Southeast Asia will likely always be a second-order interest to Northeast Asia. One American diplomat wistfully wrote us, "If others [that is, China and India] are bringing their A game to the region, we should do the same." A fair point, "should" being the operative word. Some countries are obviously more important to American interests than others. Those like Thailand and Singapore have been adept at taking advantage of our bilateral focus, helping in the war on terrorism while expanding economic ties. In the Philippines and Indonesia, we must and do cooperate in tackling entrenched problems of violent Islamic extremism. Certain Southeast Asian countries, such as Vietnam and Indonesia, because of their size, resources, and history, take on increasing importance to the United States as the region adjusts to the emergence of a powerful China. ASEAN presents a certain chicken-and-the-egg conundrum for the United States. If not for its institutional limitations, would we choose to do more with Southeast Asia multilaterally? Or does our ingrained bilateral approach simply proscribe any such outcome? For better or for worse, the United States likely will see Southeast Asia for its disparate parts for some time to come.

6

DOES DEMOCRACY COUNT
IN EAST ASIA?

*D*emocracy has come a long way in East Asia. While they differ significantly, Japan, South Korea, Taiwan, the Philippines, Thailand, and Indonesia are functioning democracies. Malaysia and Singapore might perhaps best be described as guided democracies. Seldom neat and orderly, occasionally tumultuous, sometimes regressive, they have regular elections and change governments peacefully, if occasionally turbulently, and sometimes even transfer power to the opposition. They vary in their transparency when it comes to policies and methods of governance, and each provides some degree of accountability to the governed by those doing the governing.

But the glass is also half empty. Democracy is not the predominant form of government in the region. Consider China, Vietnam, Laos, and Cambodia to say nothing of North Korea and Burma. Yet the scene is complex: even in the nondemocratic governments of China and Vietnam meaningful progress has been made, often in stops and starts, toward at least greater openness and individual freedom. Both countries, of course, have a long way to go.

The scene is also varied for those classified as democracies. Malaysia, Singapore, and even Japan are one-party states. Singapore and Malaysia do not have anything close to a free press. On the other hand, these two states have vastly improved the quality of life for their citizens. They offer a good measure of personal freedom even while maintaining tight political control. Indeed, even more than in most other East Asian countries, it can be argued that the leaders of those two countries have the best interests of their citizens at heart. Other countries of the region still have a way to go before they can claim success in establishing well functioning democracies. Indonesia, for example, has to show that its democratic institutions can generate and sustain the policies needed for economic advance, greater human security, and national unity. Until these nations make progress along that path, they remain fragile democracies.

While the peoples of South Korea, Taiwan, and the Philippines have fought hard for democracy, as one Taiwan scholar put it, "Democracy is not the only game in town in this part of the world." Democracy needs time and frequent exercise if it is to develop strong, toned muscles. It also has trouble surviving in an uncritical vacuum and benefits greatly from a free press. Civil society, also essential to democratic practice, is growing in East Asia but is undeveloped even in the democratic states. Whatever its limitations, the democratization process in the region is exciting, both to the people of the countries where it is happening, such as in Indonesia in 2004, and to democracies around the world.

Many East Asian elites, however, often regard outside efforts to promote democracy and prescribe political behavior with suspicion, even hostility, and U.S. actions in Iraq have tended to increase that suspicion. Some East Asian leaders are prone to see American pressures to open up the political process as highly destabilizing. They regard it as interference in domestic affairs and an affront to sovereignty. Asian leaders were outraged by a one-day visit of Vice President Al Gore to an APEC business summit in Kuala Lumpur in 1998 to deliver a public lecture on democracy and human rights to his host, Prime Minister Mahathir, a speech intended mostly for an American domestic political audience. Even those East Asian countries that are democratic are not inclined to proselytize in their immediate neighborhood on behalf of democracy. While confident for the most part that democracy works for them, they are much less concerned over how their neighbors are governed unless it impinges directly on them. Moreover, there is considerable skepticism that Western conceived democracy is the best political model for every state.

For example, it is widely believed in East Asia that the growth of South Korea and Taiwan would not have happened or happened as fast under democratic governments. Many Koreans, including some who struggled for democracy in the eighties, would argue that the authoritarian coup leader and later South Korean President Park Chung Hee deserves his own statue in the pantheon of economic modernizers along with China's Deng Xiaoping and Taiwan's Chiang Ching-kuo. Many in Asia look admiringly at the dramatic transformation of Chinese society and economy and conclude a democratic government could not have done it.

China's economic success often rankles American democracy proponents, who find it hard to accept that an authoritarian country economically outpaces all other countries in the world year after year. They believe it will inevitably collapse. Writings on the virtues of democracy contain important caveats regarding East Asia's examples of successful economies under nondemocratic systems. Many argue that political openness and freedom are—or will be—essential to continued economic success, even in China. But American advocates continue to be surprised by what is actually happening in China as the push-pull effect of economic success on political practice seems slow to manifest itself.

This is not the place to argue whether countries grow faster under democracy. Much depends on the quality of governance, and numerous other factors. There are also many reasons besides economic ones to argue the case for democracy. Conversely, there are all too many examples of countries under authoritarian rule that have not grown or even have regressed. Here, the point is that the case for democracy is not self-evident or deeply internalized in much of East Asia. In fact, many have tended to resent Western (that is, American) espousal of the unarguable virtues of democracy, although some East Asians—such as Anwar Ibrahim of Malaysia—argue that there are in fact such things as core democratic principles in spite of the difficulties of context. East Asian resentment helped popularize the case for "Asian values" in the decade of the nineties—societal discipline, savings, and delayed gratification. That flight to Confucianism diminished when financial disaster hit East Asia late in the decade, though it has made a small comeback with economic recovery.

As much as Americans would like to see East Asia's democratic development, the United States does not now do all that much to move it forward. For all the rhetoric of the Bush administration on democracy as the centerpiece of American foreign policy, its efforts in East Asia are small. The implementation of the American democratic vision is slow, inconsistencies are many, the resources relatively meager, and the political pressures difficult to maintain. There is also cynicism in East Asia and elsewhere that the Bush administration's dedication to democracy and its centrality in American policy blossomed only after WMD were not found in Iraq.

The volume, pitch, and cogency of our pro-democracy rhetoric rises and falls in all administrations, depending on what other issues are competing for priority on the American agenda as well as domestic political pressures. In balancing the perceived clash between long- and short-term interests in East Asia, between promoting democracy and advancing our economic and security interests, we have almost invariably come down in favor of those other interests, adding to the skepticism with which East Asians tend to regard our advocacy. At critical moments when the United States might have made a difference helping democracy along, we failed to rise to the occasion. The abortive Burmese uprising in 1988 and Hun Sen's rise to power in Cambodia in 1994 come to mind.

The ups and downs of the American commitment to democracy aside, we have to face the fact that democratic practice in East Asia will be erratic and not very pure. It occasionally seems at least a bit like our own. Many countries have taken on some of the less wholesome characteristics of twenty-first century Western democracy: the politics of division, the emphasis on celebrity, political agendas set by professional consultants, and above all dependence on money. As in the United States, money is the mother's milk of politics in most Asian countries, and it tends to empower special interests and retard meaningful reform. Corruption is another issue. It is certainly present in nondemocratic Asian governments; in China, for example, corruption is huge and an all-consuming popular issue. But corruption is also all too present in East Asian democratic governments where it erodes faith in democratic institutions and creates a vulnerability to powerful waves of populism.

Finally, there is the complicated, sometimes combustible, relationship between democracy and nationalism. Nationalism is strong in East Asian countries, democratic and nondemocratic alike. National leaders have frequently deliberately cultivated nationalism, and it has been essential to the nation-building process. Nationalism can also be a corrosive force in the neighborhood, a fertile ground for demagogy and jingoism, especially in countries where democratic tradition is not much of a rival force. One Taiwan politician nicely summed it up: "Bashing your neighbors in East Asia is a good political tactic."

Destructive nationalism in East Asia arises from a variety of causes, including territorial and maritime disputes, contentious histories, or contests for regional influence.

Nondemocratic governments frequently use nationalism and hostility toward the "other" to divert attention from their own failures and to justify authoritarian rule. As one China watcher observed, "With their type of communism, there is no cohesive force to bind the nation together. There is nationalism, but that could turn around and bite the regime. Nevertheless there's no other thing, so they're using it." Nationalism may be even more dangerous when democratic politicians use it for their own political purposes, because it has—or appears to have—greater legitimacy. Japanese politicians push nationalist themes—so far, not that successfully—by mining public resentment of what the Japanese populace increasingly regard as unfair hectoring from China and Korea about events years ago. Imagine how a freely elected democratic legislature in China might be tempted to deal with Japanese history texts or, even worse, with the Taiwan issue. All this is, of course, unknown in the United States.

THE PATHS TAKEN

The road to democracy in East Asia, like most everywhere else, has not been an easy one; nor has everyone taken the same route. In two countries—Japan after World War II and the Philippines—it had significant American content, though each nation's form has its own distinct national characteristics. In other countries, democracy largely grew out of the colonial heritage, educational institutions, and a sustained American diplomatic effort. In Northeast Asia, democratic change has often been an undulant movement away from military dominated governments. Some authoritarian military leaders like Park Chung Hee in South Korea and Chiang Ching-kuo in Taiwan helped democracy emerge by modernizing their economies. That is not to argue that democracy was their goal.

In South Korea, democratic progress was spasmodic, with a succession of coups, murders, daily student riots, and imperfect, though hotly contested, elections. In 1985, the prime minister actually warned one of us that if the American embassy invited Korean anti-military political maverick Kim Dae Jung to its annual July 4 reception, the government would actually fall. For many years, politics in South Korea were all about the dominant military trying to make sure Kim never came to power.

The remarkable Chiang Ching-kuo and other autocratic leaders in Taiwan, with the crucial assistance of an exceptionally able group of economic administrators educated in Western universities, shepherded the transformation of an authoritarian ruling party into an incarnation that eventually allowed itself to be voted out of office. Some hope this same phenomenon will be duplicated in China. We would not count on it given the fundamental differences between Taiwan then and China now, including the simple difference of size. For its part, the Chinese government is interested in improving its governance, not in creating democracy.

In Southeast Asia, the national democracy movements grew out of the independence struggles against Western colonial powers that were themselves democracies. The Dutch were pushed out of Indonesia, the British walked out of Malaysia and Singapore, and the United States wanted out of the Philippines. Indonesia has had a circuitous, often bloody, up and down odyssey from colonialism through a long period of authoritarian rule toward democracy.

Malaysia and Singapore have built conservative states on the British legacy, with a cautious commitment to more democratic practices. In Thailand, the only state in the region that had not been under foreign domination, the military ran the country for four decades either directly or from behind the curtain. To their credit—and to the credit of Thai proponents of democracy—the military came to realize that they were not capable of administering a complicated modern state. It was also clear, especially after the coup in 1991, that the Thai public was tired of them. Their political power ebbed, though not without a few hiccups. Today, under a popularly elected power-hungry prime minister, Thaksin Shinawatra, Thailand is, ironically, sliding backward in terms of democratic practice and faltering badly in handling the incendiary situation in Thailand's Muslim area. Thaksin has successfully purchased the support of the Thai countryside, but the strains his arrogant and self-serving leadership has generated are endangering his ability to govern.

The Philippines has drifted in and out of democracy, maintaining its form but often not its substance. More recently, it developed a unique method—"people power"—of getting rid of its elected presidents through action in the streets regardless of the electoral calendar. The Philippines stands as an example of the limited success of American nation-building.

The United States gets less credit than it deserves for its role in promoting democracy in Asia over the past half-century. That is largely because the route to democracy has often been circuitous and our commitment sporadic. There was a constant tension during the cold war, as there is today, between our interests in friendly authoritarian countries and our desire to prod these governments in democratic directions. Our experience in Indochina was wracked by this contradiction. The challenge of trying to build something of a democratic state in the midst of war-haunted Saigon decades ago now pervades Baghdad. For new generations in South Korea now coming of age politically and looking back on their country's journey to democracy, it sometimes appears as though the U.S. government allowed and even helped Korean military leaders to suppress popular democratic movements. Whatever the facts to the contrary, many Koreans still believe the United States supported the South Korean military in its clash with student protesters in what is known as the Kwangju Massacre in 1980, a defining moment in modern Korean history. Today, our focus on counterterrorism has perhaps become a complicating factor in countries like Indonesia, Thailand, and the Philippines, where we need cooperation from the military and police, elements of the state apparatus that are not necessarily strong advocates of democracy and human rights.

Nevertheless, whatever its warts and inconsistencies, America's diplomatic prodding, security shield, and decades of large economic and military support have helped to democratize a good bit of East Asia. Nor should it be forgotten that the United States also saved countries like South Korea from being devoured by the totalitarian North. All this effort largely preceded the proliferation inside and outside the U.S. government of the many private or quasi-private agencies dedicated to promoting democracy, open societies, and human rights abroad.

In the final analysis, democracy, of course, takes root best when it is home grown, not transplanted from abroad. Perhaps our most important contribution to democracy in Asia over the years has been to attract talented Asians to our institutions of higher education through the Fulbright Program and other government and private programs that bring potential leaders to the United States. In Asia, as well as the rest of the world, a remarkably large number of ministers, legislators, ranking officials, journalists, academics, and business leaders have American educations. Even now, despite the stringency of our visa process, Asians keep coming. In the 2004–2005 school year, some 60,000 Chinese students were registered in American colleges and universities.

To consolidate the democratic trend, many East Asian governments will need to improve their openness and accountability, show they can raise incomes, and ensure full participation in the political process by Islamic, secular, and minority groups alike. According to one young pro-democracy leader in Indonesia with whom we spoke, "Democracy does not happen with just an election. Our government has to perform . . . the popular sense is that they have not yet done so."

THE LAGGARDS

All the current laggards except Burma are communist or ex-communist states. They are the primary focus of American efforts to promote democracy in East Asia. The challenges are different in each country, since all are at different stages of development and the workings of globalization have differing effects in different countries.

NORTH KOREA

We start with North Korea, a country without even a whiff of democracy and little individual freedom, because it raises urgent problems of war, nuclear terrorism, and the risk of nuclear proliferation in Northeast Asia.

Serious movement toward democracy will not be achieved until the regime changes. That change, however remote it now seems, could occur abruptly as a result of an internal struggle or as a consequence of a wider conflict. Some assert that it could result from isolation and strong economic sanctions, but for a number of reasons noted elsewhere, we do not believe that is likely.

Internal change might also occur—and this too is problematic but more realistic—as the result of a long process of reducing hostility between North and South Korea; greater interactions with the international community; and the orchestration of economic incentives—and disincentives—to change the behavior and ultimately the nature of the North Korean government. That is the approach of China and South Korea.

It is hard to predict whether such approaches would actually lead to greater openness, better lives for the people, and fewer human rights violations. The danger is that, even if robustly implemented with skill and willingness at times to use the leverage that wealth provides, these approaches could have the perverse effect of strengthening the regime by improving its economic condition without securing any real change in its nature and providing no great material help to its people. These approaches have not attracted political support from the Bush administration, which cannot do anything about China and has not tried hard to stop Seoul's engagement policy.

No country except the United States is prepared to contemplate changing the North Korean government by force. But Kim Jong Il is not likely to go gently into the night, and North Korea has the military capability to bring catastrophe to the entire region. Nor will overthrowing the regime necessarily lead to democracy unless the country is absorbed by South Korea in a reunified Korean Peninsula.

We do not have enough information to say much about what the transfer of power to another member of the Kim family might produce, although there is little reason to believe it would be a change for the better. We also do not know enough to preclude, particularly if the regime is in serious economic trouble, a military coup, which might perhaps bring about something better than what the country has now, but is hardly likely to improve prospects for democracy.

The present American approach to political openness in North Korea, including the small number of private concerned organizations, is to focus on improving the human rights situation. It is difficult to imagine it changing the regime's behavior on this score any time soon. Activists in the Congress and a few private organizations, many devout Christians with links to South Korean religious groups, resolutely seek to expose publicly the horrible nature of the Pyongyang government, its gulags, and its massive human rights transgressions and to encourage Koreans from the North to flee the country. The U.S. government has also tried to put North Korea in the dock in every possible public forum. While producing few practical results for the North Korean people, it certainly provokes Pyongyang's rage, perhaps a good sign. Denunciations might have a little more success if North Koreans were more engaged with the outside world.

For the past five years, the U.S. government has insisted that human rights must be part of our negotiations with North Korea; it will supposedly not agree to the issue being shoved to the side as in the past. Since there have been no serious negotiations by the Bush administration on anything with North Korea until recently, it is hard to know whether this demand counts for much or is essentially rhetorical. If the United States insists on making North Korean commitments on human rights a part of an agreement on nuclear weapons, the difficulty of completing an agreement increases greatly. There also will be little we can do to hold North Korea to any commitments on human rights, other than to make it a condition for the benefits it would presumably receive in giving up its nuclear weapons programs. North Korea is not likely to allow itself to be set up in such a manner.

For its part, the South Korean government is absorbed in pursuing its engagement policy and shows little interest in human rights in North Korea or in doing much for those who flee the country. Indeed, South Korea rather fears arousing Pyongyang's anger and prefers "quiet" diplomacy, which means little happens, unless at times it is shamed into, say, accepting some refugees.

Perhaps significant improvements in the lives of at least some North Koreans might come from helping those who have fled across the border to China and live in miserable circumstances. That flow is apparently increasing. More help for this population is not likely unless China changes policy and allows international organizations like the United Nations High Commission for Refugees or interested countries or private organizations greater access to these refugee populations for material assistance or legal emigration to a third country. While China has effectively allowed many Koreans to stay in China along the border, it does not want to create incentives for others to come. China is also under North Korean pressure to stop the flow and return those who have fled.

China is not prone to bow to international pressure on Korean refugees, nor is making the issue publicly prominent, as is now being done in the United States, likely to improve their lot. Perhaps more might be accomplished with China if the United States or other countries privately sought China's support to allow more humanitarian aid agencies, Chinese or foreign, to operate quietly along the North Korean border on behalf of those fleeing. We do not say this with much confidence; moreover, it would be impossible to hide such assistance from Pyongyang for long.

BURMA (OR MYANMAR)

Because we, the authors of this book, are rather ancient, we are drawn toward using the name Burma and not Myanmar. Emotionally, we also do not like to give any sustenance to the Burmese military, which started using the name Myanmar in recent years. Burma does not exert much influence in East Asia except as an object of geopolitical rivalry or because of its export of drugs, HIV/AIDS, migrant workers, and illegal forest products. But as part of the problem of democracy and humanitarianism in East Asia, it is also important.

Much of the democratic world, including the United States, has spent the past few years preaching to the military to free Aung San Suu Kyi, the leader of Burma's major opposition party, the National League for Democracy (NLD), from house arrest. The hope has been that such pressure will begin nudging the junta toward opening a bit of democratic space. There is little to show for this effort. Aung San Suu Kyi, highly revered throughout the world, sits in effective solitary confinement, shut off from access to the outside world.

Singapore's Lee Kuan Yew once said Burma has had the worst of all worlds, socialism run by the military. Now it has only the military, but there has been little improvement. Food self-sufficiency, monies earned from exploitation of natural resources, and foreign aid enable the military to continue to run the country as it sees fit. Life for both Burmans and ethnic minorities is miserable; the quality of education has sharply declined; HIV/AIDS and malaria have infected a sizable and rapidly increasing share of the population. Burma's terrible human situation grows worse by the day.

Burma's large ethnic minority populations have been at war on and off with the central government since independence in 1948. The military repeatedly justifies its harsh rule and its vast defense expenditures as indispensable for keeping Burma together as a state. Sounds of "national reconciliation" with the ethnic groups still at war and the political parties have occasionally emanated from Rangoon since the 1988 student upheavals and the debacle of the 1990 elections. These invariably subside.

Neither exhortation nor economic pressures have so far created much incentive among Burma's military leaders to open the system or change the way they run the country. Burma's admission to ASEAN in 1997—hailed at the time for its potential for changing the country—has accomplished nothing. ASEAN's practice of see no evil, and talk about it less, has let Burma off the hook. ASEAN's surprising and successful insistence that Burma not chair ASEAN meetings in 2006 and its equally surprising criticism of the Burmese government at the ASEAN summit in December 2005 appear to be arousing the organization to do more to try to affect Burma's domestic policies.

Burma is not like North Korea. It is more open and allows many more visitors; some of its citizens can travel; and it has more connections with the rest of the world. This should create some possibility for political change, but so far, it has not worked that way. The military is deeply entrenched in the economy, making it harder to convince them to concede any power. Their iron hand keeps domestic opposition down, while external Burmese opposition groups generate little resonance inside the country. An ASEAN diplomat complained, "What can one expect from a government that moves its capital almost secretly and does not even tell its fellow ASEAN members?"

Those shaping Burmese policy in the United States are few, as is the opposition to their approach. It is an insider's issue with essentially two different approaches. The first, which is American policy, is to isolate the military government and try to bring pressures on the regime to begin serious negotiations with the political opposition led by Aung San Suu Kyi. The United States bans trade and investment (which few other governments have emulated) and mobilizes domestic and international criticism of the Burmese government. The effort has enormous support in the Congress. But it is actually dominated by a small group of legislators and their staff, whose hands are on the spigots of trade and aid. They draw support from many editorialists around the country, most notably the *Washington Post* editorial page, as well as a number of NGOs like the Open Society Institute and publicly funded private organizations like the National Endowment for Democracy. These groups support the Burmese democratic opposition inside the country as best they can, and more easily outside the country, where dedicated advocacy generally has raised the international pressures on issues related to Burma.

Although some American officials believe this "hard line" will achieve little, the Bush administration remains wedded to this approach, and there is no political incentive to change. The basic problem with this approach is that the world is divided on Burma. While the U.S. approach may deflect some countries from engagement with Burma, the Burmese military have important foreign supporters— China, India, and Thailand—who offset American economic pressures. The U.S. government recognizes that problem, and an effort is under way to have a quiet dialogue with China on Burma, hoping to enlist Beijing in urging Burma's rulers to take a different track, as the United States also tries to intensify international pressure on Burma.

The small but vocal second group, mainly in the humanitarian community and academia, argues that present policy has accomplished little while Burma continues to slide downhill. They assert that holding to the notion that the victory of Aung San Suu Kyi's party in the 1990 elections must be the point of departure for political change is a formula for stagnation. Instead, they believe that the world should stop isolating the government, seriously talk to it, and offer humanitarian assistance. These groups say that over time this approach can bring real change by showing the military that there are benefits for behaving better. Japan, Australia, and some European governments support this approach. But until Aung San Suu Kyi is released, this policy is unlikely to fly in Washington—and probably not even then.

It is hard to talk seriously about the prospects for Burmese democracy. Nor can we be confident that greater democracy would keep this ethnically fractious country together, although ceaseless military repression does not seem to have done the trick either. The world has a serious dilemma. Not to try to address Burma's awful humanitarian situation is not only obscene but detrimental to the health and well being of other nations; to accept the military rule is simply not politically feasible or desirable. Countries like India oppose isolating Burma in terms of real-politik—they believe that the world needs to engage Burma if only to diminish China's clout. No country is willing to overthrow the Burmese government by military means, although many in Rangoon's military do not believe that. Engagement is unlikely to achieve much beyond shoring up the regime, and is impossible to sell in the United States. So Burma day after day dies a little.

Diminishing the political power of the military probably requires creating fissures within the military institution itself, persuading some officers that the country is on a path to perdition and there has to be change. Indeed, a major split in the military in 2004 occurred with the fall of prime minister and intelligence chief Khin Nyunt. But we know little of the military's dynamics, and can only guess where such personnel changes may lead. On the surface, however, little has changed in the way the military controls the country. Admittedly, it is hard to test this approach but it seems, however difficult, a more practical way to proceed. One thing is certain: democracy is not on the horizon.

CHINA

We have left the mother of democracy laggards to the last. China dominates American concerns about democracy in East Asia; on human rights it has produced bruising battles within every administration. The Clinton administration, for example, started with a public determination to pressure China on human rights and democracy. It ended up with the president in China, hobnobbing with President Jiang Zemin. Democracy is obviously not the only item on our more crowded agenda with Beijing.

In some American circles, the absence of democracy in China is seen as a security issue. Defense Secretary Donald Rumsfeld publicly expresses concern about the dangers flowing from China's authoritarian rule. As China's economic growth continues and creates greater potential for expanding military capabilities, more controversy can be expected, particularly if China continues to be governed by an authoritarian Communist Party. It should be added that greater democracy may not diminish China's determination to build military power or to retake Taiwan. One does not have to go far to find democracies with an inordinate willingness to spend huge sums on their military forces and to use them.

The end of the cold war and the events at Tiananmen in 1989 changed radically the American appraisal of China. Earlier, our top leaders had expressed admiration for the strategic wisdom of Mao Zedong and Zhou Enlai, men who presided over the deaths of tens of millions of Chinese after they took power in 1949. Ironically, after 1989, the Chinese government, which was then already engineering the most positive series of changes in China of the previous two hundred years, became an institution to be reviled. The televised replay of bloodletting in Tiananmen could not be wiped away. American reaction was perhaps sharpened by the disappearance of what had seemed for a fleeting moment a viable hope for democratic pluralism in China, just as a democratic wave had built up in Eastern Europe and the Soviet Union.

But the moment passed, and circumstances changed. The nature of China's government became perhaps the biggest bone of contention between the United States and China—and it remains so today. This is not the case in the rest of Asia, where the only people expressing much concern about the way China is ruled tend to be from Taiwan and Hong Kong. China can make people rich, which for many excuses much—and also attracts many Americans. As one American businessman cynically put it, "Americans like their China democracy lite."

The Bush administration approach to promoting democracy and human rights in China has been an undulant one, much like in the Clinton administration. Enthusiasm for democracy is usually high, accompanied by much public rhetoric, at the beginning of an administration and then invariably declines as other interests take precedence. President Bush has had a little more difficulty because democracy has become his administration's flagship. Nevertheless, American administrations come to recognize with time and experience that the promotion of democracy in China is a long-term proposition, that has usually involved a variable mix of public and private rhetoric, high-level interchanges with some big-show public events, and highlighting prominent individual cases of human rights. It also includes sustained governmental support for the various programs run by NGOs and publicly funded private organizations that promote democracy. These programs encourage political openness, promote a market economy, raise political consciousness, offer differing views, and stimulate grassroots democratic sentiment. They cost little but over the longer term contribute significantly to greater openness in China and the spread of democratic ideas.

Congress is very much in the act, prodding the administration to expand democracy promotion efforts in China and to toughen its public stance on the need for political change. China is a winning political target for legislators. The U.S. education system plays a substantially more significant role, attracting tens of thousands of Chinese students, some of whom are children of high-level cadres, heightening political consciousness and encouraging them to examine the nature and limitations of their government. Democracy proponents all attest to the utility of these programs and urge more monies be devoted to such efforts. They are leaning mostly on an open door.

In China itself, economic success has brought expanding horizons, at least within the rapidly growing middle class. The growth of the private sector and the greater openness and mobility of Chinese society make people more willing to criticize the bureaucracy and condemn corruption. There is increasing focus on the glaring need to strengthen the rule of law. This same economic success also is creating sizable class differences that in themselves may be threatening to the regime's control, and the regime knows it. The bottom line—one we should not forget—is that greater pressure for internal political change is now being generated by the Chinese themselves than by outsiders. The party itself is far more sophisticated in eliciting new ideas and establishing wide international contacts. We should not delude ourselves that we are indispensable in bringing democracy to China. In the Clinton administration, an American ambassador to China was once rebuked by the secretary of state for making a similar observation about the American role. The observation may not have been compatible with Washington's approach to China at that moment, but it was accurate.

There are in China, as elsewhere, the inevitable contradictions in our approach to promoting democracy. These arise, as we have discussed in earlier chapters, from the profit motives of our companies, our need for China's cooperation in the war on terrorism and in halting North Korean nuclear weapons programs, and of course the ongoing requirement for careful management of tensions in the Taiwan Strait. Many Chinese perceive—and their government makes sure they do—that our criticism of China's political system is frequently designed to advance American goals that have little to do with promoting democracy, such as preventing other governments from selling China advanced technology or frustrating Chinese firms in their operations abroad and at home. In short, American hands are often portrayed as dirty, and our motives less than pure. Some argue that suspicions of U.S. motives in promoting democracy are now so high that we should design efforts that involve less day-to-day hectoring and more emphasis on institution building.

But there is an even more fundamental, perhaps politically incorrect, question to be asked about American efforts to promote the rapid spread of democracy in China. Is it—rapid democratization—genuinely in our interest, or in China's for that matter? Raising this issue will not buy you much in Washington other than doubt as to your sanity.

The question is not whether democracy in the end would be more desirable than what China now has. Most likely it would. Rather, the question is whether in such a huge, rapidly changing country—so difficult to run—we really know what might be the near and longer-term consequences of a serious move toward open, competitive politics. Will rapid democratic change promote continued economic progress or, by risking political and social unrest, undermine it? Severe economic disruption in China could be catastrophic for all of us. The present communist government, of course, makes this case, as it warns of the need to maintain stability. In approaching the promotion of democracy in China, a modicum of modesty, a quality not in great evidence at this time, might be in order.

The Chinese government's response to outside efforts to promote democracy now goes beyond simply stonewalling. There is a greater willingness to engage in bilateral discussions of some issues and even to allow a limited amount of alternative political activity in lower echelons. But the authorities are not hesitant to crack down hard on the press when they feel it necessary, or to continue to hide nefarious acts, as they have recently done. The leadership is certainly not prepared to go quietly despite the importuning of American conservatives. Yet, some surprising democracy projects supported by the United States and other countries are allowed to continue. Others, such as efforts to use the Internet to advance an agenda of political change, are often blocked. There is much discussion and apparently some diversity of views within top levels of the party about democracy and the pros and cons of greater political openness. Oppression, latitude of political thought, and innovation seem to commingle. We are clearly seeing political change in China and some weakening of the party's control. Perhaps the biggest question is whether the unity of the party could survive a serious economic downturn.

◆   ◆   ◆

Our pessimism about the prospects for constructive political change in Burma and North Korea is unbounded in the short term. Engagement will take a long time to work and is politically difficult. More likely, we will at some point witness a political explosion in both countries, the consequences of which are difficult to predict. Years of history will be wiped away, and the human costs can be huge.

Burma and North Korea aside, the trends within both democratic and communist-led governments in East Asia seem promising for greater openness, individual opportunity, and the expansion of democratic practices. There will of course be ups and downs. Populations and politicians are more interested in growth, corruption, and inequality, and they do not connect progress on those subjects directly to the growth of democracy. Even if democracy is not perceived as a critical issue, the public's ability to influence decisions, to understand the governing process, and to remove leaders who do not perform, clearly is.

In the critically important case of China, fear of internal breakdown will limit the pace of domestic political change. China is getting even harder to govern. On the other hand, there does seem to be a growing awareness within the Chinese leadership that popular pressure for a loosening of political control cannot simply be suppressed or bought off with more material goods. Hong Kong will pose an increasingly dangerous challenge for them as its public demands the right to elect its own representatives—a demand the leadership does not want to be heard on the mainland. Developments are pushing domestic politics in directions Americans would applaud. The more tailored, consistent, and occasionally more light-handed our approach, the more likely that we will contribute to meaningful, non-cataclysmic change.

7

WHAT DO WE DO?

"The time has come for America to formulate a coherent and comprehensive strategy to deal with the rise of Asia," a prominent Singapore diplomat and author wrote recently. We couldn't agree more. But then again, how many times since the end of the cold war have we heard such urgings from the cognoscenti about American foreign policy—in general, in East Asia, and in every other region? The task, of course, is difficult; "coherent and comprehensive" are tough standards for any foreign policy. Policy must respond to shifting forces within regions and changing priorities in the world—and contend with competing political constituencies at home. And, of course, the United States since September 11 has been absorbed by terrorism around the world and turmoil in the Middle East—no small distractions.

Throughout this book we have tried to identify the main shifts in the East Asian landscape and the issues they raise for American policy, and examine how the United States has been responding. In this chapter, we focus on what the United States should do to pursue its interests in a radically changed East Asia. U.S. leadership still remains central on major issues ranging from security to counterterrorism to trade and investment. Nevertheless, the balance of influence in the region is shifting, largely but not exclusively because of China's growing success. While American military might is still respected in East Asia, there is a growing awareness—probably more in East Asia than in the United States—that the exercise of American power is becoming more problematic and that Asians themselves must take on more responsibility for regional stability and their own well-being. East Asia has been faster than America to come to terms with an economically surging China and the economic integration of East Asia.

In a globalizing world where rapid change is a constant, it is hard to lay down broad lines of policy that are both relevant and durable, particularly when strategy seems more rhetorical than real. There is no simple set of principles, and each principle has its exceptions. Take the promotion of democracy as the supposed foundation of American foreign policy in the second Bush administration. The fact that the U.S. government says it is central and preeminent does not make it so. Promotion of democracy at times bows to other interests, such as internal stability and counterterrorism. It is not an infallible guide to policymaking, even as it shapes international perceptions. Notwithstanding their inherent limitations, however, broad policy lines are essential to orient the government, to inform the public and the rest of the world, and to show that the U.S. government knows what it is doing—even if it really doesn't.

YES, VIRGINIA, THERE IS AN EAST ASIA

Since enhanced region-wide political and economic cooperation can help preserve peace and further prosperity in East Asia, the United States should encourage the efforts of East Asian governments to facilitate regional integration and build regional institutions, including the possible creation of an East Asian Community (EAC).

Its sheer diversity—cultural, political, economic, and ethnic— makes it highly unlikely that East Asia could grow into a replica of the European Union. Nevertheless the region is coming together in ways unimaginable just a short time ago, a result largely, but not solely, of the growth and increasing openness of China's economy, which is pulling the region into an orbit of growing investment and trade. From ASEAN to ASEAN Plus Three (APT) and now to an East Asian Summit (EAS) and—perhaps one day—something that legitimately can be called an East Asian Community (EAC), the region bids likely to become a more integrated, closer cooperating entity.

While East Asian community building is inchoate and much remains to be done, the United States would be wrong to dismiss the region's efforts as insignificant or to discount their potential. *Expanded regional cooperation helps facilitate continued economic growth, reduces the possibility of conflict among the participants, helps the more backward states, and offers another vehicle for managing China's emergence as a regional and global power. It should make East Asia an even more important international player and a greater contributor to the global commonweal.*

The obstacles to an EAC are numerous. Countries are divided on what sort of EAC they want to create, who is to participate, and where the EAS and other regional institutions fit. Some, mostly in ASEAN, want American participation in any region-wide organization so as to limit China's domination of the organization and because they fear that American investment in ASEAN countries would diminish if the United States were left out. Others want an East Asian–only organization without the United States or other outside participants, believing it will become little more than a "talk shop" if they participate.

The U.S. approach toward expanded East Asian regionalism has not coalesced. Washington is watching the passing parade. Some concerned Americans fear that a region-wide organization will become a cat's paw for China and be directed against the United States, or that American trade interests will be threatened by greater East Asian cooperation. We find such fears hard to credit given the cast of characters and their enormous economic interest in protecting their relations with the United States. While a few countries see greater regional cooperation as a desirable counterweight to the United States and have become wary of an unpredictable use of American power, East Asian leaders consistently assert that they have no desire to define or posture themselves against the United States. Given the region's continuing integration into the global economy, we find it hard to believe that East Asia would not remain an open economic region.

We could do much to delay or even quash the movement if we played to the differences among East Asian countries. That would be a mistake. We should not try to force our way into the East Asian regional mix as some American officials would have us do. Nor should we try to impose our views about what countries should be included. Rather, the United States should strongly support deeper East Asian regional cooperation, including the eventual creation of an EAC, if that effort continues to take shape and gain traction. Our personal view—not a mainstream one—is that greater East Asian cohesion will advance the American interests we have cited above and is best achieved by letting East Asian countries themselves determine what sort of an EAC they want to work toward, including one that would welcome only countries of the region. We should, however, always make clear that we regard any East Asian entity as a global and trans-Pacific partner, and that greater East Asian cooperation must be consistent with the cornerstones of the international liberal economic order, including the IMF and the WTO. We also should make clear that the United States will remain heavily engaged in the region, with strong bilateral relations, a continuing security role, and regular interaction with all existing East Asian regional institutions.

East Asian countries will themselves want to maintain multilateral connections across the Pacific as they build their own regional institutions. The Asia-Pacific Economic Cooperation Forum (APEC) would seem the natural forum for trans-Pacific dialogue and cooperation. Whether this larger enterprise can take on more substance than in recent years is uncertain, but there is no harm in trying as long as APEC does not become an American device for trying to undermine East Asian community building.

The United States is accustomed to dealing with East Asian countries mostly on a bilateral basis and has come to expect a degree of deference and responsiveness to its interests. For many years, most East Asian nations have placed more emphasis on their individual ties with us than on their ties with one another. That era is slowly ending. We will be less able to rely so heavily on bilateral relationships to advance our interests. As East Asia knits together, we will want to give closer attention to the impact of our dealings with one country on our relationships with others. We will need to maintain good bilateral relations with East Asian countries, but over time we will also have to deal with East Asia as East Asia.

CHINA RISES—AND THEN RISES SOME MORE

The United States needs a clearer perspective on the implications of what is happening in China. China cannot be treated as an outlier that simply needs to complete its integration into the international system. China's rise has begun to change the system itself as well as the U.S. role in it. Given the wide ramifications of our relations, both countries have no choice but to get along with each other. The U.S. government should consistently make clear that it supports China's rapid growth, that it views China as a necessary collaborator in international affairs whatever our differences, that the United States will remain deeply engaged in East Asia, and that it will not pursue an anti-China alliance.

Getting a better handle on American policy toward China is the sine qua non for dealing with a changing East Asia. We need a vocabulary that is meaningful, and not replete with meaningless geopolitical jargon. A "unified" and even bipartisan policy would be desirable, but it is probably beyond our present political capabilities, certainly as the 2008 elections draw near.

A starting point: The United States cannot manage China, cannot control it, and cannot "contain" it. But we can and should influence it.

The Chinese giant has awoken from the slumber of two centuries. It has profound problems of governance and may stumble, but it is here to stay. The world will have to get used to that. The United States needs to approach China comprehensively as a central component of our regional and global policies. China may not be our major foreign preoccupation at this moment, but over time it will likely become such.

China has shown, so far, that it wants to work with the United States. Such sentiment, of course, may be temporary and certainly does not preclude future challenges, abrasions, and even sharp breaks on major issues. But China is well aware of its weaknesses. China also recognizes the ramified, deeper connections between our two countries and its own economic dependence on the United States. In the short term, its aspirations for international respectability and influence, including its overwhelming interest in the success of the 2008 Olympics, makes China predisposed to accommodation, not confrontation.

The Chinese are realists, and the United States needs to be realistic about China. It is a competitor of enormous potential. It is far too early, however, to conclude, as some in America have done, that the two countries are bound to be antagonists. Restraints on both sides abound. China faces huge problems in its economy and its polity. It is hard to envision how China will be governed a decade from now and what the role of the Communist Party will be. China no longer has a serious ideology. It is becoming more open but not democratic. Its long-term success—stability, greater prosperity, and hopefully the evolution of an open, more democratic system—is overwhelmingly in our interest. We should help make that happen, not work for China's failure. The collapse of the Soviet Union was the realization of our dreams; breakdown in China would damage the whole world. Meanwhile, we will have to live with a more militarily powerful China, one that is unlikely to challenge us for a long time to come but one that will have sufficient capability to give us pause, mostly on Taiwan. For the foreseeable future, we will have to maintain major military forces in Northeast Asia, and China seems in no hurry to see them depart. It would be foolish at this point to depend on China's internal politics to throw up a more democratic, conciliatory, unified government.

Nor, beyond its internal weaknesses, should we forget the restraints on China coming from its many neighbors—some quite strong and highly nationalistic. China wants and needs tranquility and stability on its periphery as it concentrates on its modernization. Its neighbors will take umbrage if China becomes too assertive or chauvinistic toward them. Some of these countries can also be expected to look to the United States for psychological and political support should China become too assertive. If that happens, our self-interest in providing such support is an important argument for our continuing diplomatic engagement and for maintaining some American forces in the area.

So how do we maintain a fundamentally decent, reasonably stable relationship with China and assert influence on its behavior? In the following ways and always with help from our friends:

First, we need to concentrate on our bilateral relationship and foster a continuing high-level dialogue on all major issues. Deputy Secretary of State Robert Zoellick has already begun doing this on a regular basis. That dialogue will have to be a long-term effort and will have to be better than most American bilateral dialogues or consultations, which have usually consisted of the United States telling its interlocutors what must be done and then waiting or not waiting for them to act. China has not accepted—and is unlikely to begin to accept—American views as revealed wisdom.

Nor will our goals be achieved by asserting that China must be a constructive stakeholder in the international system; that is, agree to abide by the rules of the system we have nurtured for more than half a century and which have served us well, except when we have decided to ignore them. Regrettably, China does not share many of our values, is not an ally, and will have its own notions of what needs to be done on major issues. That will be hard for Americans to take. Over time, China is likely to be less willing to tolerate our transgressions from some of the norms to which we are urging their adherence. This is not to say they will have better rules; most of the "rules" that we espouse on the economic side China has already accepted. We also will have to balance carefully our consideration of specific issues in terms of our overall approach to China.

None of this means we have to pull our punches. We will protect our economic interests if we can determine what they are, whacking China's practices when they deserve it and resolutely seeking change when warranted. We will need to speak forthrightly on China's affinity for the world's least savory countries, like Sudan, Zimbabwe, and Burma, although they do not seem much disposed to listen at the present time. China does not tell these countries how to behave; they let them murder their people as they choose. On some issues, the United States considers vital, such as Iran's nuclear weapons programs, our differences may well have serious and probably unavoidable repercussions on relations. We will need to be forthright and persistent on differences over human rights, democracy, and openness but cautious in our use of threats. Above all, the thrust of our dealings must be clear and reasonably consistent. To the extent we can enlist our friends and allies in a coordinated effort, we are more likely to make progress in influencing China's perspective.

Second, we must search for areas where we can seriously, not just cosmetically, cooperate. For example, given the scale and rate of growth of China's energy consumption, all countries have a major stake in China's energy policies. China, too, has a deep interest in the global energy balance. It would seem a subject tailor-made for consultation and cooperation and that in fact is beginning to occur. Nor should we rule out cooperation on security matters, bilaterally to gain greater understanding of each other's thinking, and multilaterally where our interests coincide as on getting rid of North Korea's nuclear weapons. Our two countries, however, part company on how to bring North Korea along. Nevertheless, a basis for further bilateral and multilateral dialogue has been established in the Six-Party talks.

Third, we should encourage China's more active involvement in multilateral institutions. Despite its authoritarian regime, China should be invited to affiliate in some fashion with the G-8 given its growing role in virtually all the issues considered in that forum. We should push China to take greater responsibility in international peacekeeping and to be more transparent and cooperative on health and environmental issues. We believe all this will ultimately engender more constructive Chinese involvement in the world. Promoting China's greater involvement in multilateral organs is of course a double-edged sword. We will have to listen to them and may not like what we hear. We may even have to adjust our own positions occasionally to accommodate their views.

Fourth, we will have to maintain a credible military capacity until we can better evaluate Chinese intentions. That will not be hard. China also will have to be more transparent on defense matters if it is to avoid sounding alarms in Washington and other capitals, although greater transparency will not preclude China increasing its own defense expenditures. However, the United States does not yet need to open wide the financial sluice gates for our own defense spending, although we are moving in that direction. We have considerable leverage on Beijing in many areas: they cannot, for example, resolve the Taiwan issue without us.

There is no silver bullet for dealing with China. It will require much effort, insight, and persistence; we must concentrate on the facts, not conjure up the phantoms. Obviously China too must be open to the give and take of real dialogue, not an easy matter for them. Even if we do all the above, it will not guarantee a harmonious relationship. So much can get in the way.

Managing our own domestic politics will be critical to fostering the relationship with Beijing. This will be a challenge given the myriad of conflicting interests of different American constituencies. So far, presidents have risen to the test more successfully than Congress. The current administration has held at bay most of the demands for confrontation and policies tailored to special concerns, but it is a constant struggle. Unfortunately, China does not always understand or take into account how its actions can affect the political agenda in the United States. For its part, the United States will have to choose its fights carefully with China, separating the vital from the merely important. Over time, Beijing is likely to become less willing to accommodate its economic behavior to threats of negative "congressional reaction."

The domestic politics of China are very important in its policymaking, and we need to do more to understand them. We have learned much about China, but it is not always easy to divine the internal political workings of a still secretive China, although the Chinese decisionmaking process is also becoming more transparent. At times we may even want to try to influence directly contending factions as we have long done, for example, in Japan.

DEPENDABLE JAPAN

The toughest challenge in East Asia is preventing Sino-Japanese rivalries from getting out of hand and threatening cooperation and fundamental stability in the region. The United States is crucial to avoiding such an outcome. It must be careful not to spark regional fears of a remilitarizing Japan or an anti-China alliance. At the same time, it must continue to reassure Japan about the vigor of our security alliance despite the obvious implications of China's rise for U.S. interests and policy in East Asia. Having a Japan that is more influential in East Asia is important to the United States.

Japan has been our principal East Asian ally for many years. It is an impressive power whose star faded over the past decade, and we will benefit as it regains its economic dynamism. It is natural for us to continue to have a different relationship with Tokyo than with Beijing. We share with Japan, more than with any other country in East Asia, political values and beliefs. We have compatible though not identical views on most international economic matters.

When it comes to the Sino-Japanese relationship, the United States cannot assume that common interests will overcome nationalistic tensions and moderate hostility. Since there are always dangers that political forces in both countries will play on nationalistic sentiments for short-term political gain, helping improve relations between them should be a major American preoccupation. This is not the 1930s, and there is no objective reason for deep hostility between the two countries. Certainly, Japan and China have some ongoing difficult territorial disputes in the East China Sea, but the deepening ramifications of their economic relations and other common interests are as significant as those of China and the United States.

The Japanese have never fully come to terms with the legacy of their actions in the thirties and during World War II. Other Asian nations—particularly China, despite its own sorry communist history, and South Korea—publicly view Japan as still unrepentant and unapologetic. Over the years, the United States is perceived to have abetted—or at least to have gone along with—the Japanese inclination toward circumlocution and avoidance of meaningful accountability for the past. This issue, as far as we know, has not been discussed at very high levels in our two countries. One result is that Japan's position in East Asia remains far less influential than would be expected given its huge contributions to trade and investment and the vast amount of economic aid it has provided its neighbors, including China.

We believe the U.S. government should reconsider its posture on this issue and quietly make known its unhappiness with Japan's management of the "burden of history." We should encourage Koizumi's successor to settle the Yasukuni Shrine issue once and for all with a new approach, including perhaps a new shrine with a less problematic history. It is time for more serious diplomacy. Clearly, Sino-Japanese differences will not all fade away if the Japanese prime minister stops visiting the Yasukuni Shrine. Nor is it clear that China will do much of anything in response to such a change to help mend relations. In any event, Japan will at least get off a poor policy wicket. This should help Japan shore up its position in Southeast Asia—no easy job— which should be an important part of America's attempt to help bolster the stability of that area.

As with all major countries, the principal avenues of policy are dialogue, consultation, and a search for cooperative ventures. We are used to it. We have extensive dialogue with Japan and growing dialogue with China. But there are no regular consultations with Japan and China together, which could become another useful mechanism for managing tensions between the two. China has not been interested in trilateral consultations with the United States and Japan, probably fearing that as allies we might gang up on China. Many Americans and Japanese have been urging the three governments to have such talks, but never succeeded in arousing much enthusiasm among officials. As China prospers and gains confidence, however, China's attitude may change. A major initiative is required to get such an effort under way: the president should invite the Japanese and Chinese leaders to meet with him early in 2007 in the United States or East Asia to review outstanding issues in the region. This will likely cause consternation in the rest of East Asia. Some countries, like South Korea, will not like being left out, others will inveigh against a big-power condominium, but we believe this would be an important step forward in big power relations.

We should avoid stimulating—even inadvertently—competition between China and Japan by word or deed. We want to avoid concerns in China or elsewhere that we envision a Japanese military buildup as a means to contain China. While Japan has serious security interests in Taiwan and wants the island to remain separate from China, we should resist the temptation to bring Japan any further into the Taiwan problem or to seek from Japan public comments and support. Nor do we want to give encouragement to those forces in Japan that advocate a much more assertive approach to becoming a "normal" state and so urge Japan to shed major constraints on its military policies.

Japan has the economic weight and technological capability to become a major military power and quickly produce nuclear weapons. The Japanese public has not wanted to go down that dangerous road. We want to preserve that sentiment even as Japanese concerns about China and threats from North Korea tend to erode it. Beyond providing for its own defense, we see no great purpose served by Japan taking on expanded security responsibilities globally and regionally, except in close collaboration with the United States and the United Nations. Japan can and certainly should contribute even more to international peacekeeping. We believe it is important that the United States seriously search for a way to make Japan a permanent member of the UN Security Council soon. It certainly deserves it.

The United States must now look beyond the Koizumi era, which is drawing to an end, and the seemingly close Bush-Koizumi relationship, to the long-term management of relations. We will need to recognize that the Japanese public does not necessarily go along with the recent fulsome rhetoric of the two governments about the relationship. We will have to accept that Japan's Iraq deployment will almost certainly end, perhaps as early as 2006. Moreover, the Bush administration, after five years, has still not resolved politically tough problems such as Okinawa basing. Japan's need for energy may make Japan, like China, a difficult partner in dealing with Iran. While the bilateral relationship should remain strong whatever the problems, it will likely require a lot more tending in the coming years.

YES, ONE KOREA—BUT WHEN?

We should push ahead to negotiate the best possible nuclear agreement with North Korea in the Six-Party forum, but, given the nature of the North Korean regime, we need a longer-term strategy for dealing with the chronic threat from a failing but dangerous state. That approach should be based on working with South Korea and China to try persistently to draw North Korea out of isolation and open up possibilities for internal change. For example, the United States should push to open liaison offices with the clear intent of establishing diplomatic relations; we should offer to bring students here for study; and we should open talks on the lifting of economic sanctions and building trade ties even as we pursue a nuclear weapons agreement.

If there are lessons to be learned from the past decade, the first is that we have to deal with North Korea as it is and that waiting for it to collapse is not a policy. Another lesson is that a nuclear agreement, while crucial, is not by itself sufficient for ending the long-term threat from a dangerous and untrustworthy country. A third lesson is that our approach must be acceptable to the other principal concerned powers of the region, especially South Korea and China.

We welcomed the Bush administration's decision last year to talk directly with North Korea about a deal to end its nuclear weapons programs. Along with many others, we conclude that negotiations are the only feasible way to end the North Korean nuclear threat.

Economic pressures and isolation have little bite against a country prepared to limit its interaction with the world severely and one whose rulers do not shy from imposing great hardship on its population. Moreover, China and South Korea have made it clear they will not go along with such policies or with military options. It is far from certain, however, that an agreement will be concluded.

Whether Pyongyang and Washington have made the strategic decisions needed to reach a deal remains to be seen. For Washington, the main questions for reaching a satisfactory deal are who goes first in carrying out the required elements of an agreement and how much ambiguity can be tolerated in verifying North Korea's compliance with a pledge to abandon nuclear weapons and efforts to build them. An important political consideration for the administration is how to justify a quid pro quo deal with Pyongyang to its domestic political base, one that would require the United States to do what it has done before but usually calls by another name, buy them off. For Kim Jong Il the strategic questions are whether he is prepared to live without the deterrent of having nuclear weapons or at least being able to say he has them and how attractive are the benefits of an agreement.

However unappealing it may be to deal with North Korea, we cannot see any alternative given the constraints posed by America's friends and allies. The United States should pursue its own strategy of engagement—albeit conditioned engagement—with Pyongyang. We have much that Pyongyang needs, including, most importantly, our political recognition, the lifting of economic sanctions, and acceptance of its entry into international financial institutions. In contrast to South Korea, however, our goal would not be reconciliation with North Korea. Rather, we would seek to foster internal changes in North Korea that could lead to changes in external policy—relating concrete benefits to concrete change. The goal of such conditional engagement would be to weave an ever-thickening web of connections between North Korea and the rest of the world that would contribute to the greater opening of the country and create an interest in better behavior, including compliance with its obligations in a nuclear agreement. Such an effort also means making sure that South Korea stops subverting nuclear negotiations by continuing to open its pocketbook too widely, giving North Korea the benefits it would obtain through a nuclear agreement without having to give up its weapons programs.

The difficulty of implementing such a strategy is enormous. We would have to overcome the North Korean tendency to reject conditionality and to pick and choose among international connections. We would have to prevent North Korea from simply pocketing everything offered while doing little to increase transparency and confidence in its compliance with a nuclear agreement. We would have to coordinate such an approach closely with South Korea, especially regarding what we each require from Pyongyang. Such an approach would encounter stiff resistance in the United States; powerful forces reject any support for North Korea that would appear to countenance that regime's profound mistreatment of its own population.

The only thing such a policy of conditional engagement has going for it is that it is better than the alternatives that we have previously discussed. It is the only approach that would not bring us into a collision with South Korea. Moreover, it fits with both China and South Korea's engagement policy.

We have not yet sufficiently departed from reality to believe that the approach we propose will win the support of the Bush administration. We all may have to wait until a new administration is in place for this sort of change in Korean policy.

North Korea remains in serious domestic trouble. We may be seeing a bit more realism—the signs are still contradictory—on the part of Pyongyang about its plight, which could produce more flexibility in its approach to the outside world. Nevertheless, there is an inherent tension between North Korea's need to open to the world in order to improve its economic situation and the regime's fear that exposing its populace to greater contact with the outside poses major risk to its survival. China certainly took that risk. Given its economic support and considerable influence in North Korea, China can be crucial to the opening of North Korea, and indeed, the success of its economic model may still be the biggest inducement to change in Pyongyang. In the end, regime survival will remain the litmus test against which Kim Jong Il will measure his options. In the case of the United States, Kim Jong Il may come to believe he is better off waiting out the Bush administration.

The United States also should support Korean unification and refrain from substituting our judgment for South Korea's on how best to achieve that goal. Unification will occur some time—some assert it is already happening—but how or when no one can predict.

We believe it is more likely to occur abruptly as a result of break-down in North Korea than as the outcome of any unification strategy. In the meantime, South Korea's use of its economic power to improve connectedness with the North and create dependency, and the less bellicose tone of South-North relations, have made war on the peninsula less likely though far from inconceivable.

There remains a dangerous contingency. If the Six-Party talks continue without positive results, the Bush administration will face a major political and strategic dilemma. Will it do nothing and simply accept North Korea continuing to build its nuclear arsenal, or will it proceed—unilaterally, if necessary—to a much tougher approach to stop Pyongyang's nuclear weapons programs? That could lead to a major confrontation with friends and foes alike, another reason for a determined negotiating effort.

The U.S.–South Korean relationship is in serious trouble despite the rhetoric coming from both governments. We can continue with different approaches for some time given the common concerns of both countries about a North Korean attack. But if we want to preserve the alliance for a long time to come, we have to try seriously to heal the breach; that may also have to wait until 2009.

TAIWAN—THE OTHER POTENTIAL FLASH POINT

The United States should defend the status quo by continuing to emphasize to Taiwan that independence is not an acceptable goal and that any effort in that direction endangers U.S. interests. It should strengthen the status quo by trying to rein in the arms race in the Taiwan Strait. It also should make clear to China that its present terms for settlement are not enough to encourage Taiwan to begin serious negotiations.

The United States has lived with the Taiwan dispute for so long that there is a tendency to accept it as a permanent feature of the landscape and assume that whatever scares the two sides periodically create will ultimately fade away. Our posture derives in great part from confidence that neither side really wants a devastating and costly war, our sympathy for a democratic Taiwan, and from the domestic political difficulties we would face if we tried to change policy. So the drama appears to have an unending number of scenes, though one day perhaps the audience (us) may decide to go home.

It is hard not to be for Taiwan—a David versus Goliath situation. The people of Taiwan deserve great praise: they have built an impressive economy, fought hard for democracy, and understandably want their own little space in the sun not controlled by repressive autocrats who have never set foot on the island. But U.S. policy has to be made with our heads as well as our hearts.

Taiwan counted for more in the United States when Mao was around, China was weak, and outsiders were shaking their heads about the Cultural Revolution. That era is long gone, and China's influence and power have grown, while political support for Taiwan around the world continues to decline. Few countries want to risk Beijing's wrath by speaking up for Taiwan independence, no matter how democratic Taiwan is. Many oppose a Chinese takeover of the island, but few, if any, would do anything about it. Time is not, we believe, on Taiwan's side. Taiwan's hope is that China will weaken or implode—or that it will simply not be willing to incur the cost of forceful unification. Taiwan's interest should be more in buying time, not tweaking the dragon.

We have a somewhat contradictory scenario of expanding economic ties between Taiwan and the mainland, and a growing arms race by the United States and Taiwan with China. It is not politically correct to acknowledge it publicly, but the continuous military buildup by the parties may actually result over time in a decline in the effectiveness of the American deterrent, while imposing an ever increasing monetary cost on Taiwan, which has to face U.S. wrath if it declines to purchase the weapons the United States is offering. We are skeptical that more weaponry will produce more bargaining power, greater confidence for Taiwan, or deterrence against Beijing. But the United States cannot get off this train.

The most difficult challenge to the status quo will come from Taiwan's politics. The U.S. government must continue to impress on Taipei that it cannot take steps or employ rhetoric designed to lead to independence, or in the current diplomatic parlance to "unilaterally change the status quo." President Bush has forcefully done this, but time passes, politics change, and nothing should be taken for granted. Indeed, Taiwan's democratic politics may actually be in the process of changing. On the other hand, if the opposition Kuomintang Party—more amenable to dealing with Beijing—returns to power in Taiwan's 2008 presidential election, as seems quite possible at this point, that might lead to more promising possibilities for serious cross-strait negotiations. However, prior to that election, there will be a protracted and perhaps dangerous political struggle in Taiwan, in which we may at times have to make our views loudly known. Chen Shui-bian is making the United States go through such a period as of this writing.

So far Beijing has shown little interest in making new negotiating proposals; nor is it clear that Taipei wants a deal. Despite our urgings, Beijing will not talk to the present Taiwan government. We should leave no doubt in Beijing that Taipei cannot accept the Chinese offer of "one country, two systems," and that China has to make better proposals across the board that might encourage Taiwan to begin serious negotiations. It is not clear what those proposals should be, perhaps at some stage some sort of confederation. So far Beijing has shown little interest in putting forth any new proposals. At some point, the United States might feel the compulsion to get involved more directly in brokering a solution—something less than independence but more than "one country, two systems." That day has not yet arrived.

If we have not already done so privately, we should try to engage China in serious discussion on restraining the arms race in the area. That will probably not elicit much interest from Beijing, which will insist on maintaining an effective deterrent to Taiwan independence, but we should persist. A dialogue on that score may at least clean up misconceptions.

Southeast Asia Once Again

The United States should continue to help the countries in the region prevent jihadist activity; it should join with ASEAN to try to improve the performance of its weaker states; and it should focus its bilateral energies on building up Vietnam and Indonesia to ensure their growth and the region's independence and stability.

Southeast Asia is once more on our radar screen. Our substantial economic ties alone give us a stake in the region's success, and the threats of terrorism in parts of the region have raised that stake. In addition, a plethora of dangerous problems—from piracy to global public health, most notably HIV/AIDS and Avian Flu—demands our active cooperation with countries in the region, which would be significantly enhanced if the problems could be handled on a multilateral basis. While the region does not hold the strategic importance of Northeast Asia, its prosperity and independence are essential to our interests in the stability of the region.

China's influence in Southeast Asia will continue to increase. It will not control these countries, but they will be more and more sensitive to China's views on important issues. China will continue to do things we do not like, such as bolstering the Burmese junta. We do not need to get into head to head competition with China in the region, but neither do we want our influence to recede. U.S. efforts should focus on helping Southeast Asian countries maintain their growth, improve their governance and cohesion, and preserve their freedom of action. We should encourage their deeper and wider political and economic cooperation within the region and with all countries of East Asia, including China.

For the most part the governments of the region realize that eradicating jihadist violence is important to their well-being and the success of their economic modernization efforts, including attracting foreign investment. The United States has accomplished much in fighting jihadism through improved cooperation with intelligence and law enforcement agencies. But pockets of extremism remain, and terrorism erupts with alarming frequency. Each country will have to be dealt with differently. For example, while we strengthen our counterterrorism cooperation with Southeast Asian countries, we must take care not to give a good housekeeping seal of approval to countries like Thailand for ill-conceived and badly implemented counterterrorism efforts, which by all accounts have inflamed sectarian conflict in its three southern Muslim provinces.

ASEAN's greatest shortcoming probably has been its failure to do much to improve the lot of its poorest members. The United States should encourage and provide resources to aid ASEAN's efforts to improve laggard members like Cambodia, Laos, and Vietnam, and it should encourage the richer countries of Northeast Asia also to work toward that goal. Such an objective should be a central part of the U.S.-ASEAN dialogue.

There are signs that ASEAN patience with Burma may be running out, and we should encourage this pressure on the junta. We should encourage ASEAN to appoint a special envoy with the task of talking to Beijing and New Delhi, urging them to use their influence with the Burmese government. Bringing about real improvement in that country simply may not be possible at this time. It will likely, in the end, require help from China, which will be hard to get but worth pursuing. We must, however, take action with other countries to tackle the badly declining humanitarian situation in Burma instead of just talking about it, and that means some serious dealings with the government.

However important our efforts to strengthen Southeast Asia's regional identity and cooperation, power still lies with its individual member states. Most importantly we and our friends need to strengthen our ties with the two largest, most independent, but very poor states in the area—Vietnam and Indonesia—and help spur their economic growth.

WHITHER THE SEVENTH FLEET?

For the foreseeable future, the U.S. bilateral alliances and military forces in Northeast Asia remain essential to peace and stability in East Asia. In addition, we should cultivate stronger security relationships in Southeast Asia, although we see no need for permanent installations there. Our emphasis should be on establishing overall closer relations in the region. We should move when propitious to transform the Six-Party mechanism into a permanent security consultative organ, with or without North Korea.

One of the constants in East Asia since World War II has been the presence of a large and powerful American military force in the Western Pacific and East Asia. Our forces have been reduced and reorganized over time but remain potent. More generally, many in East Asia, even in those countries that are sometimes suspicious of American motives, still see U.S. forces as a "stabilizing" element in the region. Even Beijing recognizes a link between keeping American forces and alliances in the region and avoiding the still remote possibility of Japanese nuclear armament. The American military also has proven its worth as an agent of humanitarian assistance during the tsunami disaster.

As long as the Taiwan issue remains unresolved and there is a need for deterrence against a North Korean attack on the South, the United States should not consider the withdrawal of its forces in the region. That posture still remains widely accepted politically in the United States.

Far reaching, overdue organizational changes in U.S. forces in both Japan and South Korea are under way. Some in the policy community want to reduce forces further as part of the global repositioning of the American military, some as punishment of South Korea for differing with us on how to deal with North Korea. But more unilateral force reductions tend to undermine our other efforts on the peninsula, including the nuclear weapons negotiations. We also should enhance our security relations with Indonesia and Vietnam, including the provision of appropriate military equipment and training to Jakarta.

Assuming that both the Taiwan Strait and the Korean Peninsula some day—probably not too soon—will be crises of the past, we will then have to reexamine our military presence in East Asia and the Western Pacific. It is not too early to think about this issue and what sort of security arrangements will be most appropriate if that occurs. The biggest question will be the future of our forces in South Korea and perhaps Japan. It is not clear to us that trying to perpetuate an American military presence in South Korea is appropriate or even possible.

While we want to maintain our military-to-military relationships in the area, we must continue to look beyond bilateral military ties to find a pragmatic, constructive, and multilateral security framework. American initiative is essential to such an effort. Obvious starting points are a U.S.-Japan-China dialogue and a transformation of the Six-Party mechanism into a permanent security consultative dialogue.

PROMOTING DEMOCRACY

The United States should put more resources to promoting democracy in countries where it does not exist, like China; to helping to consolidate it in those countries where it is weak and still at risk, like Indonesia; and to trying to improve it in those that fail the test of good governance, like the Philippines. In authoritarian countries, like

Vietnam, emphasis on promoting market and intellectual openness will be more fruitful than democracy promotion for the short term. Democracy-promotion efforts in general should include concerted help to strengthen governance and civil society and build institutional capacities in weak states.

East Asia is slowly moving in the direction of democracy. We believe America's democracy-promotion efforts have been helpful in China and resonate widely because of the Internet and other channels of communication. Progress is not linear or uniform, however, and there will continue to be ups and downs. We need a varied approach, particularly for China and Vietnam; one size clearly does not fit all. It will take time to develop democratic habits in societies that have had quite different systems of government. Our support can bolster this process, but the drive for democracy must emerge primarily from within each country. Chinese democracy with Chinese characteristics will be worth waiting for. We need to help stimulate it.

For the less economically developed countries, like Cambodia, we should emphasize human rights and better governance. For the hard cases, like Burma and North Korea, our choices are limited. Little will happen while the current governments remain in control. Reconsideration of how we deal with both countries, particularly North Korea, and what we can achieve is in order, but our democratic politics currently preclude it. Peaceful regime change is obviously difficult, but essential. Continuing to highlight our concerns about human rights and providing humanitarian support is about as much as we can do under current ways of thinking. For countries like Vietnam, democracy is not the first task; we should stress human rights, intellectual openness, and the adoption of the Chinese economic model.

Efforts to promote democracy, including those managed by nongovernmental agencies, are important to our interests in East Asia. We should expand them and enlist support from other countries in the region as much as possible. We also need to reduce the cynicism associated with U.S. efforts to promote democracy, no easy task. To do that, we have to make clear to others where we stand and be candid with ourselves about where we can do some good and where we cannot. Our policies must strike a balance: promotion of democracy is a prominent goal, but it is not a preeminent one and we should not be gilding the lily. Keeping nascent democracies like Indonesia afloat is a long-term and formidable task. Managing expectations about our role in promoting democracy is a challenge not only in the countries where we are involved but, perhaps, most of all in the United States itself.

HOW THEY SEE US—DOES IT MATTER?

The stature of the United States in East Asia is diminished. It is probably recoverable in most places, but that will take time, particularly in Muslim countries. Rebuilding our image will depend not only on how we explain our policies, but obviously on the policies themselves. Displaying less certitude about the correctness of our judgments and more willingness to give serious consideration to the views of others would serve us well in the long run—an obvious but often forgotten point.

Elites in East Asia, other than business ones, do not hold a positive view of the United States. To be sure, there has always been grumbling and nationalistic resentment about America and its domination of the region. But the rising tide of skepticism—even antagonism—one now finds in the region marks a dramatic reversal from the respect and admiration the United States enjoyed in most East Asian countries from World War II to the end of the cold war.

The invasion of Iraq and our policies in the Middle East continue to fuel animosities, even in non-Muslim countries. Perhaps more important is an apparently growing conviction within the region that all that matters to the United States is what it wants and that it is insensitive, even indifferent, to what other countries prefer. As one Chinese academic observed to us, "For Washington, it's either their way or the highway."

The perceived American tendency to be indifferent to the wishes and needs of others is only part of the problem. The preeminence we are determined to exercise and preserve is feeding opposition to American policies. As our insightful Singaporean diplomat wrote, "Americans don't understand the extent to which American power intrudes into the existence of others. We come up against American power—all types of power—every day. It touches our lives all the time and we really don't like it." His words are a little over the top, but he makes a point.

This may be a passing phenomenon. People and countries in the end respond to what the United States does today, not what it did yesterday. But these animosities could be somewhat longer lasting, in part because they are held most strongly by East Asia's younger generations and are not just a reaction against what is frequently described as the overweening arrogance of the Bush administration. They are also rooted in a long-standing perception that the United States believes that only it knows what is best for the rest of the world and what is best for it is best for everyone. It is not easy to manage the consequences of policies believed to have been misguided that produce vast unintended consequences. Popular animosity to American policies will have greater consequences for our interests as East Asian governments become more democratic and more attentive to public opinion.

Also worrying is that we are no longer sufficiently replenishing the East Asian intellectual capital in the United States. We have benefited for many years from the fact that many of East Asia's leaders in business, academia, and government came to the United States for their education. They have been invaluable assets in promoting understanding about the United States in the region. We obviously have new security concerns following September 11, but we need to keep in mind our interest in continuing to attract East Asia's best and brightest to our universities, which means that we should continue to reassess our visa requirements and financial support. We should put more emphasis and more funding into intellectual exchanges, including for example the Fulbright program. Fortunately, that need appears to be increasingly recognized in the U.S. government.

◆ ◆ ◆

East Asia is on the cusp of further great advances. With Japanese economic resurgence under way, East Asia may well become the most dynamic area of the global economy. The region is certain to become a much bigger player in world affairs, something the United States will find it hard to adjust to. The challenge will not be met by threats and imprecations, by homilies to the Chinese from American leaders, or by diatribes from our legislators. Our power remains great, but it will be tested in fundamental ways, though probably not on the battlefield. No country can substitute for the United States in keeping the peace. But maintaining the peace and also advancing our interests in East Asia requires insight, wise policy, and a new willingness to listen to others in the region, some of whom will not always accept our views. It also requires a better understanding of the forces of change in East Asia, the new context in which we find ourselves, and the limitations of military force. None of this should be beyond us.

Acknowledgments

We are indebted to many, many people in the United States and East Asia who talked to us about the major issues raised in this book. The book simply could not have been written without them, their insights, and their views of the policy problems. We were particularly blessed by the candor they brought to our discussions. We forgo listing them, which would take two or three pages. We also owe great gratitude to the numerous embassies, hosting organizations, and private companies who provided food, forums, and very helpful intellectual exchange during our travels to the region.

We do, however, want to single out those charitable souls who were prepared to read all or part of the text. They provided a superb unpaid critical service above and beyond the call of friendship, given their own very busy lives. They were very blunt in correcting many errors and misconceptions. We not infrequently appropriated some of their thinking. Whatever this book's limitations they made it better. They are of course not responsible for any of our remaining errors and certainly not its shortcomings. And so to Alan Romberg, Richard Solomon, Ambassador Chan Heng Chee, Michael Abramowitz, Yoichi Funabashi, Jusuf Wanandi, Ambassador Ralph Boyce, Don Emmerson, Michael Armacost, Sophie Richardson, Stephen Solarz, Mark Abramowitz, Richard C. Leone, Ellen Bork, H. Allan Holmes, Michele Bohana, Brian Joseph, Don Xia, and Roderick MacFarquhar we give our deep thanks. We thank Veton Surroi of Pristina for generating the nice part of the title.

We owe probably our greatest debt for getting this book done to Jessica Gingerich, our superb research associate, editor, writer, recorder, and administrator. She may have read this book ten to fifteen times over a period of six months. She handled all our incessant requests with great skill and no complaints. She was quite simply indispensable.

We want to thank Richard C. Leone, president of The Century Foundation, for his very strong support of our effort and his endurance in seeing it through to publication. Our thanks also to Carol Starmack for her unfailing help in getting all the things we needed, and to Beverly Goldberg, our excellent and remarkably patient editor and her editorial assistant Tom Helleberg. Laura Newland, with The Century Foundation's Washington office, was enormously helpful in preparing the manuscript for publication and giving some excellent unsolicited editing of the text. Claude Goodwin provided numerous outstanding covers including the last one.

At the Fletcher School we want to thank Melissa Tritter profusely for her outstanding research help and for being a wonderful scribe, critic, and manager of our long trip to Northeast Asia, and Alison Jarrett, who also provided excellent research support.

Last, but certainly not least, we owe a great debt to Sheppie Abramowitz and Chris Bosworth for their unending support and encouragement and for putting up with endless groans, sighs, and general complaining.

INDEX

ABOUT THE AUTHORS

MORTON ABRAMOWITZ is a senior fellow at The Century Foundation. He has formerly served as president of the Carnegie Endowment for International Peace; acting president of the International Crisis Group; ambassador to Turkey; assistant secretary of state for intelligence and research; United States ambassador to the Mutual and Balanced Force Reduction Negotiations in Vienna; ambassador to Thailand; deputy assistant secretary of defense for inter-American, East Asian, and Pacific affairs; special assistant to the secretary of defense; and special assistant to the deputy secretary of state. He is the coauthor, with Richard Moorsteen, of *Remaking China Policy* (1971); author of *China: Can We Have a Policy?* (1997); and editor of *Turkey's Transformation and American Policy* (2000) and *The United States and Turkey: Allies in Need* (2003).

STEPHEN BOSWORTH is the dean of the Fletcher School of Law and Diplomacy at Tufts University. Previously, he has served as ambassador to the Republic of Korea; executive director of the Korean Peninsula Energy Development Organization; president of the United States Japan Foundation; ambassador to Tunisia; ambassador to the Philippines; and as director of policy planning, principal deputy assistant secretary of state for inter-American affairs, and deputy assistant secretary for economic affairs at the State Department. He is coauthor, with Morton Abramowitz, of *The Pacific Community: American Myth? Asian Reality?* (1996).